STUDIES IN HISTORY, ECONOMICS AND PUBLIC LAW

EDITED BY THE FACULTY OF POLITICAL SCIENCE OF
COLUMBIA UNIVERSITY

Number 343

AN HYPOTHESIS OF POPULATION GROWTH

AN HYPOTHESIS OF POPULATION GROWTH

BY

EZRA BOWEN

AMS PRESS
NEW YORK

094481~~2~~

~~98458~~

COLUMBIA UNIVERSITY
STUDIES IN THE
SOCIAL SCIENCES

343

The Series was formerly known as *Studies in History,
Economics and Public Law.*

Reprinted with the permission of Columbia University Press
From the edition of 1931, New York
First AMS EDITION published 1968
Manufactured in the United States of America

Library of Congress Catalogue Card Number: 68-58550

AMS PRESS, INC.
New York, N.Y. 10003

To

CAROLINE BABCOCK BOWEN

PREFACE

THE simple formula to which the principles of population have been reduced in the pages that follow is not offered in total or partial refutation of earlier writers. *It is contended merely that forces and influences operating upon the growth of population may be reduced to two overwhelmingly significant—and perhaps all-inclusive—factors, wealth and living-standards, and that a formula predicated on those two factors should prove helpful in promoting an understanding of the intricacies of population growth.*

In his preface to Mr. H. Wright's essay on *Population,* Mr. J. M. Keynes says in explaining the author's aim:

His object will have been accomplished if he can do something to direct the thoughts of a few more students to what is going to be not merely an economist's problem, but, in the near future, the greatest of social questions,—a question which will arouse some of the deepest instincts and emotions of men, and about which feeling may run as passionately as in earlier struggles between religions. A great transition in human history will have begun when civilized man endeavors to assume conscious control in his own hands away from the blind instinct of mere predominant survival.

Professor E. M. East of Harvard University prefaces his recent essay on population, *Mankind at the Crossroads,* as follows:

The study of the question was first undertaken without reference to its importance in the broad sense, the relation of the increase of population to the ability of population to sustain itself, but rather because it came to the forefront of every problem of human heredity, of every question of social hygiene, of every investigation into physical welfare of the people individually and collectively.

7

And in the opening chapter of his *Population and the Social System,* Nitti says, " All other questions of economics, whether those regarding distribution, or those concerning the production of wealth, are secondary as compared with the problem of population, or rather, are but aspects, as it were, of a vast prism." Here we have an English economist and publicist, an American physiologist, and an Italian statesman and economist testifying unreservedly to the extreme significance of the topic of population.

Recognition of the significance of our topic is not new. *The Quarterly Review* for April, 1830, says:

If there ever was a subject exceeding all others in general importance, and in which a right or wrong conclusion may most materially influence the destinies of mankind—if there ever was a question demanding for its discussion, beyond all others, the most calm and candid deliberation, the completest freedom from all party or personal feelings, and an earnest and philosophical desire to search after Truth, and truth exclusively—this is that subject—this is that question.

The author's principal aim throughout the pages that follow is elevated to a moderate angle. It is calculated to carry no farther than a thorough examination of the possibility of reducing the complex of population principles to a simple and enlightening pattern of formula.

The author owes profound thanks to: Professors Wesley C. Mitchell, Robert Emmet Chaddock, J. M. Clark, Vladimir G. Simkhovitch, Edwin R. A. Seligman and the late Henry R. Seager, of Columbia University. He is deeply obliged also to Professor James H. S. Bossard of the University of Pennsylvania and to Doctor B. W. Kunkle, Professor of Biology at Lafayette College.

E. B.

1931

CONTENTS

CHAPTER I

A FORMULA OF POPULATION GROWTH

HEREDITY is one half the plan of biologic progress. Variety is the other half. Progress (or adaptation to environment) appears in the scheme, however, only because of *propagation beyond the means of subsistence*—with the consequent, premature distruction of individuals that are in general the least fit. That idea, propagation beyond the means of subsistence, is the vital part of the Darwin-Wallace theory of automatic, biologic progress. That belongs to Malthus.

In developing their scheme of biologic progress—which they considered an explanation of species, but which modern biologists refuse to accept upon that footing—Wallace and Darwin grasped the principle of heredity, the principle without which chaos and confusion would possess the bio-universe. At the same time they observed that within the bounds set by heredity there are infinite, individual deviations, the principle of variety—a principle without which progress is impossible, for progress implies difference. (There are, of course, many persons who believe that all progress is mere difference—or change.) But these two principles, heredity and variation, which were the whole of the early capital of Darwin and Wallace, are but the inert ground-work of a theory of biologic progress. They are its indispensable prerequisites, but alone, they are dead and without consequence; and they might have remained so for long had they not been fertilized and enlivened by the Malthusian idea, over-propagation.

This theory of progress through over-propagation results in two opposed doctrines of population; the political and the economic. The political doctrine exhorts man to propagate and prevail; the economic to be cautious and comfortable. Among the lower orders of animal life, where propagation rates are large and where the destruction of life is correspondingly great, it is plain that the political doctrine is the more practicable. Offspring appear in millions. Group survival is the result of prolificness. Billions of individuals perish prematurely, but the kind continues.

It is only lately that man has been differently situated. In recent centuries however the man kind has everywhere prevailed over all others—even over the bacilli of typhoid fever and diptheria. In the words of the Eden legend, man has been fruitful, he has multiplied, he has replenished the earth, he has subdued it. Man has subdued beast, reptile, insect and bacterium. He need fear, today, only the more predatory of his own kind. Yet the age-long doctrine prevails, reason has tempered only slightly the innate tendency to over-propagate.

Only a few years ago, Nature was depicted everywhere as full-breasted, smiling, generous, protective, cornucopia in hand—the nature of Rousseau, of Locke, of William Godwin. Then came a shrewd London broker turned philosopher and a country parson—David Ricardo and Thomas Robert Malthus—these thoughtful men called sharply into doubt the orthodox conception of an inexhaustibly bountiful Nature; they were the first writers to emphasize, in the general scheme of man's relations with nature, the universal part played by *scarcity*. Thenceforth there gradually crept into human thought the conception of a niggardly, pinching, treacherous nature, written with a small *n*, a nature that may or may not count every sparrow that falls to the ground, but one which in any case does very little about it: a nature that puts diptheria bacilli in everyone's throat, there to await a moment of fatigue and depletion to begin a massed attack upon one's life : a nature that starves every appetite and puts a penalty upon the lucky satisfaction of desire.[1] This idea of universal scarcity gave off a wholly new and unaccustomed light; most men refused to look within the circle of its radiance; but it revealed to a thinking few the biologic and economic realities behind the doctrine of human damnation.

Propagation beyond the means of subsistence meant that, beyond all doubt, the yoke of desperate toil was firmly and, presumably, forever fastened upon the neck of man. " In the sweat of his face " must be eat bread. Why did not man, " the thinking animal ", see through the grim but thin drollery of his ever humorous creator? Nothing could be more apparent than the direct relationship between over-propagation, poverty and misery. Then why has man been so slow, so timorous, in stopping the rising flood of humanity when intelligent people everywhere understand the divine, the immemorial, hoax from school days? Man is the cowardly animal, as becomes a small beast, lacking horns, tusks and talons : a few hundred thousand life cycles of virtual defenselessness have taught him that caution nearly always pays. Nevertheless, throughout the Western Civilization birth rates are declining sharply. Man is not becoming less prolific (nor is woman) ; by simple, mechanical means he is stopping the flooding tide of human increase and casting off the curse of Eden.

Population growth and poverty are, in broad meaning, simply the upper and lower millstones of human life—of human happiness. Attempts to increase the well-being of mankind are almost certain to prove fruitless unless the growth of population is taken into account. No social, eco-

[1] *Cf.* Ross, E. A., *Scientific Monthly*, vol. xxiv, p. 265.

nomic or political program can be laid out with any large degree of justifiable hope until the factors that lie beneath, and govern, population growth have been uncovered, defined and arranged to form a rough, simple, working explanation, a hypothesis, of the mode of human increase.

.   .   .   .

Populations tend to increase as aggregate wealth increases and tend to decline in numbers as standards of living rise. Here is a formula of population growth expressed in two coordinate clauses. It suggests that one variable (size of population) is controlled by two other variables, (wealth and the living-standard). The dependent variable, size of population, *tends* to move in the same direction as the second variable, wealth and it *tends* to move in a direction opposite to movements of the third variable, the prevailing standard of living.[1]

Among social scientists the terms *standard of living, scale of living, living-standard,* and *plane of living* all signify of course the general level of material well-being, an economic concept; but as with nearly all economic concepts it refers to

[1] It may be properly objected that our formula as stated in this first, introductory chapter is a mere truism. But it is perhaps not purely captious or entirely unnecessary to point out that—*by definition*—any truth once clearly stated becomes a truism and that, nowhere in the literature of population growth, from Malthus to East and Pearl, does there appear evidence of constant consciousness of the " obvious truth " (truism) stated here. The quotations from authorities, presented near the end of Chapter XV, were assembled from an almost exhaustive survey of the entire literature of population; they appeared originally as mere flashes, fragments of sentences or at best single sentences, gleaned from four to seven hundred page volumes. But the strength of our formula need not rest entirely upon its value as a clear, complete statement of a fundamental economic truth, an economic truism; a significant psycho-economic relationship lies beneath its surface: the supply side of population growth is determined overwhelmingly by the *desire* for higher living-standards. This point is developed in Chapters XIII, XIV and XV, especially Chapter XV.

something which has a large psychological content. Among classes or groups within a community standards of living differ, but when the term is preceded by the definite article, it may be taken to mean, the characteristic annual consumption of goods by efficiently maintained families of the laboring class.[1]

Although Darwin's main thesis—progress and species arise from propagation beyond the means of subsistence—has been importantly reshaped, the fact of over-propagation, upon which this thesis rests, has stood up under the scrutiny of four generations of biologists. It is today one of the central axioms, theories, hypotheses, prejudices—call it what you will—of every biologist: *All life tends constantly to press upon the conditions of existence.* Collective life, everywhere and always, tends to exceed the warrant for it. And this, it appears, is simply the converse of the first clause of our formula or hypothesis: " Populations tend to increase as aggregate wealth increases."

It is not the increase of populations however that needs explaining. The universal tendency to over-propagate, coupled with an enormous and cumulative expansion in human well-being, amply justifies a far greater growth than any population has experienced. " Assuming a doubling in twenty-five-year periods, to be well within the historic as well as the physiological limit, the descendants of a single pair living at the time of Christ would today be sufficiently num-

[1] It is perhaps too confusing to point out in the text of this earliest chapter that our hypothesis has two phases: one, a purely economic, which which should in time appear as a truism (illustrated below in the " ant instance ") and two, a psycho-economic phase. As will appear later, actual family size is determined by *the desire* for higher standards of living. The desire for greater self-expression, which, in our current civilization is limited almost entirely by economic status, is the *motive* that controls family size. Our justification for not making a split statement of the formula (to include both phases) is that the desire for a higher standard of living is in direct proportion to the height of living-standards.

erous so that the entire surface of the earth would furnish
standing room for about one-eleventh of their number." [1]
It is the slowness of population growth and the small size of
present-day populations that want explaining.   Here then is
offered the possibility of an important economy of attention.
We may concentrate mainly upon the second clause of our
formula: populations tend " to decline in numbers as living-
standards rise."   Our main task is to examine the proposition that rising standards of living, in their complete bearing, explain a curious slowness in the growth of modern
populations.

In brief, the problem of population presents two sharp,
clear questions: (1) Why do populations increase?   (2)
Why do they not increase more rapidly?   Biologists have
answered the first question with unanimity, offering propositions that are supported by an assuring array of data.
Students of population however answer the second question
with widely diverging opinions.   Do the valid portions of
all of these opinions find their ultimate explanation in the
rising standard of living?   Upon this quintessential putting
of the question the main weight of our investigation must
fall.

The working of our formula, or hypothesis, may be illustrated by an imaginary instance from insect life and some
rough data of population and human well-being:—a tiny
colony of ants appears in a desk drawer.   A few grains of
sugar at tea time somehow fell there and attracted these immigrants.   There was food in the region from which they
came, but it was not so plentiful as in their New World.
Just so has America, for example, become peopled with
Europeans.   An ant, let us say, requires for sustenance, one
grain of sugar a day.   We supply, daily, exactly ten grains;
the ant population soon will settle down to exactly ten.   If

[1] Reuter, E. B., *Population Problems*, Philadelphia, 1923.

there were originally thirteen ants, three must emigrate or die. There are precisely ten grains of sugar, and that will support ten ants—no more. The rate of propagation is a furious one. That matters not. Ants in other regions get wind of the sugar, and a terrific immigration sets in. Again, no matter. Immigration, emigration, death rates, birth rates—all are secondary considerations in the population problem; they are themselves determined mainly by economic circumstance. The controlling fact is the sugar supply, ten grains—that settles it: a population of ten, yesterday, today, forever. . . .[1] The population of Nevada per square mile amounts to seven-tenths of a person. Nevada's meagerness will support no more. But Massachusetts' humming mill-wheels produce a flow of wealth that supports a population per square mile of four hundred and seventy-nine. More sugar, more ants.

In a burst of open-handedness, we raise the sugar ration to twenty grains. A few weeks later we take a census—and with what result? To be sure: twenty ants. There was immigration, but no matter; the death rate slackened; it is quite possible that even the birth rate may have changed—biologists are not quite clear on that point—but no matter. There is but one matter of import: twenty grains of sugar daily instead of ten.

For hundreds of generations the population of North America (before Columbus) remained nearly stationary at a million and a half.[2] Today, only four and a half centuries later, it is a hundred times as great. A vast wilder-

---

[1] This ant instance—and the material which follows—is not introduced of course to substantiate our thesis, but merely by way of illustration. A physicist exhibiting a model—made of wire and wooden balls—representing the relative positions of the protons and electrons of a chlorine atom and their paths of motion, is not proving a theory of matter, but simply illustrating an extremely compelling hypothesis.

[2] Carr-Saunders, A. M., *The Population Problem*, London, 1922, p. 477.

ness for thousands of years yielded to bow-and-arrow sustenance enough for a million and a half of mankind—no more. Then forests were felled, making rich tillage and pasturage. Machinery came, and system, and science, opening richer fields: coal fields, oil fields, iron fields, copper fields, gold fields. A Niagara of wealth poured forth its abundance. Population increased a hundredfold. More grains of sugar: more ants.

Let us see how our little colony is getting on: twenty grains of sugar, daily, and twenty ants. However absurd, let us say that our ants demand a bird-shot each to roll about in play. No; our generosity will not afford so much. But as they insist we compromise on ten shot, and daily, ten grains of sugar. Ten grains of sugar and twenty ants? Yes; ten ants must die. A standard of living that includes both sustenance and play pinches out ten lives. High and unbalanced living-standards are as deadly as natural scarcities.

Cruelly high standards of living check the growth of population as effectively as ever did niggardly nature. In modern communities of Western civilization there are families possessing an automobile whose children are not properly clothed, or nourished, or doctored. Dressed to look like bankers' sons, young men stand on street corners in winter smoking cigarettes to keep warm, because they have no money for woolen underwear and top coats. Handsome coupes which flash through fashionable boulevards on pleasant Sunday afternoons, are not all occupied by rising young attorneys and plant managers, but often a clerk from a department store or a bank. Painfully, week by week, that clerk is paying something down to an automobile dealer as the price of his Sunday masquerade. At first glance, huge modern wealth seems to have lifted man above the reach of the relentless claw of natural selection, but the burden of a towering standard of living bears him down. The family of the modern wage-earner whose wants and worries include theatre tickets, a motor car, satin slippers and radio can afford little thought of physical examination or oculist or dentist. Twenty-five percent of the children in our large cities go to school every day badly nourished (in New York thirty-four per cent) and the parents of many of them own motor cars, radio outfits, fur coats—at least one of these luxuries.[1]

Had our colony of ants been content with five shot for play and fifteen grains of sugar, the population could have been maintained at fifteen. Had they insisted upon their shot and other gimcracks besides, driving us to cut the ration to five sugar grains, the surviving ants might have lived a well-equipped, civilized, sophisticated life; but survivors would number only five. . . . The example is absurd?—It is not true to ant life? No, but true to man life, where interest is thus divided between desires and needs.

A wren, a mouse, a perch—every living thing but man—has a fixed standard of living: food every so often, crude shelter perhaps, and nothing further. With these lower creatures, an increase in sustenance means a proportionate increase in population. But man produces consciously a large part of the food values he consumes, and he insists upon producing and consuming other values as well. (The value of a motor-car, a very ordinary motor-car—that value, in simple food, would support a family for seven years.) Man's productive energy is divided: part is expended upon the production of food values, and part upon the production of far different values: buildings and clothes, steamships and railways, theatres and parks, telephones and talking pictures, radios and motor-cars, smoking material and chewing gum.

[1] Bossard, J. H. S., *Problems of Social Well-Being*, New York, 1927, p. 96.

In the proportion that these things enter into the standard of living—by just so much, the tendency of human populations to increase as wealth increases is thwarted. Populations, whether of ants or wolves or butterflies or men, tend to increase directly as wealth (weal) increases; but when speaking particularly of man, one must add: population tends to decrease as the standard of living—and with it, the standard of craving—rises.

Though the annual flow of wealth in Great Britain more than equals the total wealth produced each year in China, the population of Great Britain is but forty million, and the population of China, perhaps four hundred million. A vast difference in the plane of living explains this striking contrast: the Chinese standard of living is hardly a tenth as high as the British. The population of the United States totals one hundred and twenty million, and, though the rate of wealth production is not nearly as great in India, numbers there far exceed the population of the United States. Again, a difference in the plane of living will explain. If America were to convert into food values the huge flow of wealth that they create, contenting themselves with an East Indian scale of living, population might expand to a half a billion—assuming, of course, a revolution in food-producing methods in the United States or in some dark continent with whom America might exchange her manufactured goods—and this assumption is not nearly so bold as the suggestion that an American be content with a standard of living cut to a tenth its present height.[1]

The amount of wealth produced annually in Montana is

[1] These generalizations, drawn from the "commodity level" of analysis, are of course far too rough for any but illustrative purposes. The effect of different price levels obtaining in the regions named—a significant consideration—has been ignored only to achieve clarity at the outset of our attempted synthesis of population principles.

about equalled in Mississippi: but Mississippi has three times Montana's population. Simply, the plane of living in the southern black belt is very low. Standards of living on the other hand are about the same in Idaho and Kansas; yet Kansas' population is four times that of Idaho. And why? Kansas produces annually far more wealth than does Idaho. If the annual production of wealth in Great Britain increases by ten per cent, but every family consumes ten per cent more in comforts or in luxuries, population must remain the same.

Birth rates, death rates, immigration, emigration—all are secondary considerations in the population problem. The piston, piston-rod and crank-shaft of a steam engine are important but secondary circumstances; the underlying matter is the pressure and expansive force of steam. Controlling factors in the growth of human populations are but two: the rate of wealth production and the standard of living.

"What all strive for, even the poorest, is not a living but a way of living." [1] Here is an appealing view that is slowly pervading thought upon the problem of population. David Ricardo was one of the first persons to appreciate in the slightest the bearing of the standard of living upon the size of populations; he says: "The friends of humanity cannot but wish that in all countries the labouring classes should have a taste for comforts and enjoyments, and that they should be stimulated by all legal means in their exertions to procure them. There cannot be a better security against a superabundant population.." The second clause of our hypothesis, which hazards the guess that population varies inversely with the prevailing standard of living, is simply an acknowledgment that these views are probably correct.

The modern struggle for higher and higher living-standards not only delays marriage slightly and brings a sharp re-

[1] MacIver, R. M., "Civilization and Population", *New Republic*, December 2, 1925.

striction of births, it causes a disregard of the fundamental necessities of life. Everyone is swept into the race for civilization's prizes; the pace becomes so furious, and attention is so intently centered upon winning the distinction lent by the latest model this or that, or the elation and thrill to be had from the newest form, or pitch, of amusement that there is starvation in the midst of plenty. The desirability of good food and other essentials is through its very obviousness thrust into some oubliette of consciousness; while luxuries, which are the more conspicious for their rarity, are feverishly desired. Under-nourishment, exposure and resulting diseases are as definitely—though far less fully—operative in checking the growth of population as when wealth was less abundant.

There can be no quarrel with the desire for higher living-standards. The standard of living furnishes in fact the most positive and definite measure of human happiness. Furthermore, the large probability is that higher standards of living are as inevitable as they are good. It is contended here merely that if standards of living increase more rapidly than wealth, population must, quite obviously, decline.

In wording our hypothesis, have we used the term *wealth* correctly? Do we mean wealth or do we mean well-being? —Populations tend to increase directly with wealth, or, Populations tend to increase directly with well-being? There is an important difference in meaning—in part these terms are contradictory. Wealth is a smaller realm within the domain of well-being. Human wealth comprises all items of well-being that exist under scarcity conditions. A clear warrant certainly for saying that these terms are in large sense contradictory, for only when an item in human well-being becomes inadequate—becomes scarce—is it classed as wealth. That area in the field of well-being not covered by the term wealth, comprises items of well-being which do not exist under scarcity conditions, and which therefore cannot constitute a limiting, or a controlling, circumstance. We have chosen our language accurately: Population tends to vary directly with wealth. *Wealth* is our word.

Let us sum up: The tendency to overpropogate is universal. Life everywhere presses closely the conditions of existence. Human life is no exception. Wealth—all items of human well-being that exist under scarcity conditions—epitomizes the prime limiting circumstances of population growth. The growth of population has not, however, kept pace with amelioration of the conditions of human existence—populations have not increased as fast as wealth. How can one to explain the apparent *slowness* of population growth? The sole difference between the human case and all other cases in population growth is a cumulative inclusion of new items in swiftly rising living-standards. Wealth multiplies rapidly, but it is split into ever larger shares. A certain increase in wealth does not result therefore in a proportionate increase in population. Marriage is delayed slightly and births are restricted. Furthermore, emphasis is thrown upon non-essential values, and the simple necessities of life are neglected: undernourishment, exposure—and resultant diseases—are consequently kept in play. A rising standard of living tends to trim population at both ends; it reduces birth rates sharply and, to the extent that it is unbalanced, it works against the fullest possible reduction of the death rate. Our hypothesis of the growth of human populations should therefore read:—*Populations tend to increase, directly with wealth, and inversely with prevailing levels of living-standards.*[1]

[1] Throughout this chapter, and in later chapters, "unbalanced" standards of living are referred to directly and by implication. Standards of living may be unbalanced of course in an infinitely, or indefinitely, great number of ways; but in its bearing upon population growth (or restric-

tion) an unbalanced standard means particularly one into which mainly ego-satisfying goods enter to the prejudice of those goods essential to the maintenance of an efficient physical being—though it is not to be denied, certainly, that some minimum amount of *self*-satisfaction is probably essential to physical well-being.

CHAPTER II

MALTHUS, A REVALUATION

SYSTEMATIC thought upon the subject of population growth did not begin with Malthus. Earlier than the writings of the Mercantilists however, coherent statements upon that subject were largely the propagandistic pronouncements of political and religions bodies, and they throw almost no light upon the probable value of the hypothesis we are engaged in examining. The Mercantilists prescribed expanding populations. The rise of great powers and the rise of Mercantilism are merely the commercial and political aspects of one and the same phenomenon: huge states competing for control of the ultimate sources of the material good things of life and for the privilege of exploiting the alleged backward peoples of the world. For three hundred years the pale men of the earth outdid each other in seizing and in plundering. All this took men and money, but mainly men. The sages of the hour, who for the first time in the history of the world were in their several individualities one and the same person with the merchant princes, wrote very engaging essays setting forth the glories of large families. William the Third, heeding their advice, taxed bachelors, as did Colbert—Louis XIV's unexampled master of extortion. Prussian law required the marriage of males before their twenty-fifth year—and subsidized the institution. Maria Theresa of Austria broke tradition and permitted solders to marry. In 1767, she decreed a bounty to sergeants, corporals and common soldiers of three kreutzers a day for each legitimate child. British colonial legislation had a like inclination; for example, the colony of Maryland enacted that unmarried men, more than twenty-five years old, and childless widowers of the same age should pay in certain circumstances, a tax to be applied to the support of foundlings.

Writers and theorists to justify these programs were not wanting. The motive expressed in theory and practice alike was plainly the outcome of a nationalization of the " instinct " of self-preservation, a desire for world dominance, a militaristic doctrine; argument nevertheless ran in economic terms. Theorists, doctrinaires, and writers noted that where wealth was abundant there were people in great numbers, and they came by an easy pathway to the conclusion that more people meant more wealth, that if a nation or a great city wished to be wealthy it must encourage the multiplication of population. The fundamental and significant truth of the matter runs of course in a direction precisely opposite to their stream of thought. Wealth or abundant opportunities for the development of wealth draws an abundant population.

John Graunt (1620-1674) in his *Natural and Political Observation Upon the Bills of Mortality* says,

Now forasmuch as princes are not only powerful but rich according to the number of their people (hands being the father as lands are the mother and womb of wealth) it is no wonder why states by encouraging marriage and hindering licentiousness advance their own interest as well as preserve the laws of God from contempt and violation.

Sir William Petty (1623-1687) spoke unmistakably in favor of the multiplication of population, and considered it the most significant mark of prosperity. In his *Political Arithmetic,* he recognized a relationship between the growth of wealth and the growth of population. In his *Treatise of*

Taxes and *Contribution,* he associates population and wealth more definitely, giving population a causal character. "Fewness of people is a real poverty," says this noble scholar, " and a nation wherein are eight millions of people is more than twice as rich as the same scope of land wherein are four." John Locke seconds his opinion—though Locke's vigorous individualism made him more nearly the father of the natural liberty or physiocratic school of econo- mists than a follower of the Mercantilists, from whose logic physiocracy was in part of course a reaction.

Thomas Mun (1571-1641), a merchant prince and popu- lar pundit of political economy, was one with his Mercantil- ist colleagues in advocating swarming populations: " For when the people are many and the arts are good, there the traffic must be great and the country rich." [1] Samuel Fort- rey (1622-1681) and Sir William Temple (1628-1699) follow the crowd: " The true and natural wealth of nations," says Temple, " is the number of people in proportion to the compass of the ground they inhabit." [2] Sir Joshua Child (1630-1699) was an ardent believer in the advantages of a swarming population. He felt quite certain that an increase in numbers meant an increase in riches, and that a dwindling population foretold poverty.

In brief, the Mercantilists recognized a direct relationship between population and wealth, but they centered attention upon national wealth and neglected the general level of in- dividual welfare. They arrived in consequence at popula- tion theories which omitted entirely the role played by stan- dards of living. Davenant, Derham and Adam Smith, however, seem each to have gained a progressively clearer insight into the direct relationship between wealth and num-

[1] Mun, Sir Thomas, *England's Treasure in Foreign Trade,* p. 12.

[2] Temple, Sir William, " An Essay Upon the Advancement of Trade in Ireland," vol. iii, p. 6 of *Works* (1757 ed.).

bers and the concurrent, inverse relationship between numbers and the desire for higher living-standards.

Benjamin Franklin, who was born an Englishman and by
treason became an American citizen, was in thought and
spirit often a Frenchman. Nowhere—not even in America—was Franklin so fully appreciated as in France. He
was greatly influenced by the current school of French economists, the Physiocrats. This great American sage, in his
*Observation Concerning The Increase of Mankind and the
Peopling of Countries* says something which sounds very
much like Malthus:

There is no bound to the prolific nature of plants or animals,
but what is made by their crowding and interfering with each
other's means of subsistence. Were the face of the earth
vacant of other plants, it might be gradually sowed with one
kind only, as, for instance, with fennel; and were it empty of
other inhabitants, it might in a few ages be replenished from
one nation only, as, for instance, with Englishmen.

Here undoubtedly is the most significant writing upon the
subject of population, or upon the broader subject of biology, before Malthus; for Franklin's principle, if not the
actual progenitor of the cataclysmic ideas of Malthus, Darwin and Wallace, contained a clear suggestion of their
essential element.

In 1776, the first year of American independence and the
year of the first practical substitution of steam power for
manual labor, Adam Smith issued his great work, *The
Wealth of Nations.* Smith, like Holy Writ, is notorious
for furnishing quotations to any devil who passes: directly
or indirectly much of the thunder of Robertus and Marx is
derived from the *Wealth of Nations,* but that same book has
been a rich source of reactionary doctrine in every land.
Smith's views upon population possess this same dual
character.

In the main however Adam Smith takes the view of the out-and-out mercantilist, the militarist, the churchman: " The most decisive mark of the prosperity of any country is the increase in the number of its inhabitants." Further on however, we find the slightly Malthusian pronouncement: " Countries are populous, not in proportion to the number of people whom its produce can clothe and lodge, but in proportion to that of those whom it can feed "; and then, what seems to be the very essence of Malthus' essay, " Every species of animals naturally multiplies in proportion to the means of their subsistence and no species can ever multiply beyond it." As an effective basis for the Darwinian hypothesis this statement is however wholly inadequate. In fact, it carries no slightest implication of the essence of the Malthusian thesis. Malthus contended that all life forms have a constant tendency to multiply *beyond* " the means of their sustenance." Whereas Smith, repeating himself in substance later, says, " No species can ever multiply beyond the means of their subsistence." This was the last significant voice heard before 1798 when Malthus uttered his great essay on the principle of population.

Hume, Wallace, Franklin and Adam Smith—these were teachers of Malthus, but pupil exceeded masters. It was William Godwin however, that latter-day saint and proponent of perfection, who incited the ordinarily mild Mr. Malthus to argue warmly upon the population problem with his father—an ardent Godwinite and a follower of Rousseau. The elder Malthus and Godwin, with their salient and distressing optimism, stirred young Thomas Robert Malthus to an astounding vigor of thought and clarity of expression. His written refutation of their view is perhaps—if we remember the debt of Darwin and Wallace—the most influential piece of writing ever committed to paper; for upon its central thesis (Life everywhere tends to exceed the warrant for it.) rest basal propositions in nearly all departments of modern thought.

William Godwin, author of the Enquirer, may perhaps be fairly called a thoroughgoing optimist. Let the reader judge from a page of his *Political Justice*. There is a paragraph to the effect that the time may come when we shall be so full of life that we need not sleep and so full of living that we need not die; the need of marriage will be superseded by the diversion of developing the intellect; we shall be as angels; and then,

Other improvements may be expected to keep pace with those of health and longevity. There will be no war, no crimes, no administration of justice, as it is called, and no government. Besides this, there will be neither disease, anguish, melancholy, nor resentment. Every man will seek with ineffable ardour the good of all.[1]

It was a—possibly unworthy—desire to puncture this gorgeous bubble that brought forth, in 1798, Malthus' first essay on the *Principle of Population*.[2]

A modest country parson, Malthus called down upon his head a stream of vituperation sufficient to sink a navy. Nevertheless it did not occur to any contributing to this torrent that a fire which could not be put out with a smaller stream must be the very fire of truth itself. The quiet rural scholar and parson, was accused of defending smallpox, slavery and child-murder; of denouncing soup-kitchens, early marriage and parish allowances; of having the impudence to marry after preaching against the evil of families; of thinking the world so badly governed that the best actions

[1] Godwin, William, *Political Justice*, bk. viii, ch. ix, p. 528, London, 1793.

[2] Brown, Ford K., *Life of William Godwin*, London, 1926, p. 124.

do the most harm; in fine, of taking from life all of its joys and virtues.[1]

Thomas Robert Malthus was the son of a radically inclined English country gentleman, who was the friend of Rousseau and executor of his estate: Daniel Malthus was—rarest of creatures—a gentle optimist, nevertheless an admirer of that rampant optimist, William Godwin. The Malthuses, father and son, were fond of polemics, and, by the fireside or while taking walks, often had a friendly bout of argument. When Godwin brought out the *Enquirer* in 1797, the debate blazed up.

The younger Malthus, affirming as great love for humanity as ever his father had—or Godwin, or Rousseau, or Condorcet—protested that he could not acquire " that command over his understanding, which would enable him to believe what he wished, without evidence, or to refuse his assent to what might be unpleasing when accompanied with evidence." [2] He was what the American philosopher, William James, called tough-minded, in contradiction to tender-minded, the quality of being convinced by words grammatically and rhetorically expressed, regardless of import. So he opposed vigorously the parental view—impregnated with the lofty philosophy of Rousseau, Condorcet and Godwin.

Being of a serious and economical turn of mind, to see his carefully worked out and earnestly expressed ideas disappear into thin air was distasteful, so he wrote,

The following Essay owes its origin to a conversation with a friend, on the subject of Mr. Godwin's Essay, on avarice and profusion, in his Enquirer. The discussion started the general question of the future improvement of society; and the Author

[1] *Edinburgh Review*, vol. 64, January, 1837, art. ix.

[2] Malthus, T. R., *The Principle of Population*, preface to first edition, London, 1798.

at first sat down with an intention of merely stating his thoughts to his friend, upon paper, in a clearer manner than he thought he could do, in conversation. But as the subject opened upon him, some ideas occurred, which he did not recollect to have met with before; and as he conceived, that every, the least light, on a topic so generally interesting, might be received with candour, he determined to put his thoughts in a form for publication.[1]

The full title of the thesis which followed was, *An Essay on the Principle of Population as It Affects the Future Improvement of Society, With Remarks on the Speculation of Mr. Godwin, M. Condorcet and Other Writers.*

The essay was published anonymously. It was instantly recognized as a significant piece of writing. Enemies attacked it only with their stoutest cudgels. Friends found it quite capable of defending itself. William Pitt, the Prime Minister, paid it the rarest, if not the greatest compliment a piece of philosophy has ever received; he put its principle immediately into political practice; he dropped his bill to amend the Poor Law.

At this notable reception no one was so surprised as Malthus himself. He busied about trying to find how much there really was in this principle of population which he had so cursorily pronounced. To his astonishment he found that much had been written upon the subject. Bashfully he inserts in the preface of the second edition (referring of course to the first essay) " It was written on the spur of the occasion, and from the few materials which were then within my reach in a country situation. The only authors from whose writings I had deduced the principle, which formed the main argument of the essay, were Hume, Wallace, Dr. Adam Smith, and Dr. Price." [2]

[1] Malthus, T. R., *The Principle of Population*, preface to first edition, London, 1798.

[2] Malthus, T. R., *The Principle of Population*, preface to second edition, London, 1803.

Six editions of the essay were published during Malthus' life-time. Between the first and second editions there were more than a score of formal replies. Discussion appeared also in public journals, and in parliamentary debate, but—as with many great and astonishing books—it seemed that almost no one read it. Even N. W. Senior, England's most distinguished economist of his day, confessed that he trusted more to his ears than to his eyes for a knowledge of Malthusian doctrine, though he had written a learned dessertation upon the followers and critics of Malthus.[1] *The Edinburgh Review, Or Critical Journal For April 1810 . . . August 1810* says, " The excellent work of Mr. Malthus, though it has certainly produced a great and salutary impression on the public mind, appears to us to have been much more generally talked of than read, and more generally read than understood."

Like every popular conflict, however fundamental or simple the issue, the Malthusian controversy has been hopelessly muddled from the beginning. Early critics and opponents of Malthus, after the manner of popular critics, attacked not his main proposition but the consequences which they saw flowing from it. A few critics were led even so far away from serious discussion and sound science as to put into practice the immemorial first axiom of jury lawyers: When you have no case, abuse the plaintiff's attorney—and in this case Malthus was his own attorney. Cobbett made himself prominent among early critics by inventing the sobriquet ' Parson ' Malthus. It occurs in the following passage in which Cobbett addresses a young farmer:

" Why " said I, " how many children do you reckon to have had at last? "

" I do not care how many," said the man, " God never sends mouths without sending meat."

[1] Bonar, J., *Malthus and His Work*, New York, 1924, p. 3.

" Did you never hear," said I, " of one Parson Malthus? "
" No, sir."

" If he were to hear of your works, he would be outrageous, for he wants an Act of Parliament to prevent poor people from marrying young, and from having such lots of children."

" Oh, the brute," exclaimed the wife, while the husband laughed, thinking I was joking.

There was however one capital misunderstanding—one that, apparently, existed even in the mind of Malthus himself: *The Malthusian theory, as viewed through a vista of one-hundred and forty years, and in the light of subsequent developments in economic and biologic sciences, is not a theory of population but a theory of poverty.* One need not marvel however that the author of a significant piece of scientific work can mistake its fundamental meaning, for, if uncommon, it is not unheard of. Did not the revolutionary Darwin persist to the day of his death in calling his great book the *Origin of Species?* Biologists everywhere accept Darwin's *Origin of Species* almost *in toto* as a hypothesis, or as a theory, of biologic progress; but an increasing number of first rate biologists find that it does *not* explain the origin of species.

No superficial reading or hearsay evidence of the thoughts of Malthus reveals his central proposition—as even recent criticism plainly shows—for the overwhelming majority of anti-Malthusians attack his statement that population increases in geometric ratio while the supply of human aliment increases in arithmetic ratio. Quite true, the dogma of the ratios occupies a prominent position in *The Principle of Population*—and he stuck to it through six editions, but it is far from being the central meaning of his great essay. No one who has read him through the six editions published during his lifetime, or even through the pivotal first, second and sixth editions could possibly mistake the essential and

surviving meaning of his work: Life, everywhere and always tends to exceed the warrant for it. Wallace did not
mistake this matter, nor did Darwin; and it is rather too bad
that the perspicacity of recent students has not been capable
of penetrating this extremely perspicuous book. Speaking
of the *Principle of Population,* Wallace says, " It was the
first work I had yet read treating any of the problems of
philosophical biology, and its main principles remained with
me as a permanent possession, and twenty years later gave
me the long-sought clue to the effective agent in the evolution of organic species." Darwin writes,

In October, 1838, that is fifteen months after I had begun my
systematic enquiry, I happened to read for amusement Malthus
on population, and being well prepared to appreciate the struggle
for existence which everywhere goes on, . . . it at once struck
me that under these circumstances favorable variations would
tend to be preserved and unfavorable ones to be destroyed.
The result of this would be the formation of a new species.
Here then I had at last got a theory by which to work.

The first edition of Malthus' essay begins, " I think I may
fairly make two postulata:
" First, That Food is necessary to the existence of man.
" Secondly, That the passion between the sexes is necessary,
and will remain nearly in its present state." These are propositions which, for historic reaches of time, even the most
finical will admit as axioms. They do not however, necessarily produce the proposition which Malthus brings forward as his third siege gun: " Assuming, then my postulata
as granted, I say, that the power of population is indefinitely
greater than the power in the earth to produce subsistence
for man." Then comes the joy and delight of captious critics, the straw man which they hurl to the flames, and call it
scorching Malthus: " Population, when unchecked, increases
in a geometrical ratio. Subsistence only increases in an

arithmetical ratio. A slight acquaintance with numbers will show the immensity of the first power in comparison of the second." Now having fired what he thought were his three heaviest guns, but which even his most loving friends today know were but bursting paper bags, he utters a statement which brought to a majority of intelligent human beings an entirely new way of looking at life:

Through the animal and vegetable kingdoms, nature has scattered the seeds of life abroad with the most profuse and liberal hand. She has been comparatively sparing in the room, and the nourishment necessary to rear them. The germs of existence contained in this spot of earth, with ample food, and ample room to expand in, would fill millions of worlds in the course of a few thousand years. Necessity, that imperious, all-pervading law of nature, restrains them within the prescribed bounds. The race of plants and the race of animals shrink under this great restrictive law. And the race of man cannot, by any efforts of reason, escape from it. Among plants and animals its effects are waste of seed, sickness, and premature death. Among mankind, misery and vice.

This reduced to a simplest term, is the essential Malthusian proposition. This is the spark of living fire which set Wallace and Darwin aglow to light less penetrating minds through the labryinthic bio-universe. Reducing Malthus' statement to a minimum—even at the risk of bungling—it runs: Life everywhere and always tends to exceed the warrant for it, with consequent universal suffering and destruction. Any one who refutes this, refutes Malthus: persons attacking the essay at other points merely indulge in wooden sword play.

The next step in Malthus' reasoning is along the path of clear logic: If the population everywhere and always tends to exceed the warrant for it, there must be constant checks upon its growth. He then goes through the motions of dis-

covering these checks and naming them. The " ultimate
check' is the scarcity of food; in general however, this
check is seldom reached. The " immediate checks " are diseases and harmful customs, resulting directly and indirectly
from food shortage. These " immediate checks " fall into
two groups, " positive " and " preventive." The positive
checks are unwholesome occupations, severe labor, extreme
poverty, diseases, bad nursing, war, plague and famine.
The preventive checks are moral restraint and vice.

In his thoroughgoing book on *Malthus and His Work,*
James Bonar develops the Malthusian thesis in a way that
does not in the slightest prelude the outline just given: Bonar
finds that Malthus, despairing to master all forms of evil,
confines his study to one, the tendency of living beings to
increase beyond the available food supply. He then goes
on to show how under Malthus' treatment this apparently
simple idea, over-propagation, becomes two collateral propositions. In the case of plants and animals, reason does not
come into play; new lives are crowded into the world only
to be wiped out by starvation. The struggle is for room and
food. An individual survives only through ability to crowd
his fellows into oblivion. But man is more happily endowed: the instinct for reproduction is equally strong, but he
does not blindly follow it; he asks himself whether he may
not be bringing into the world beings for whom he cannot
provide. If he sweeps reason aside, he tends to increase his
numbers beyond the means of subsistence, and his numbers
must be cut down to those limits by suffering and starvation.

An interesting explanation of the mathematical language
in which Malthus expressed what he considered to be his
principal thesis is offered by Bonar:—Malthus maintains
that population increases by itself, but food is increased by
an agency external to it, the human beings that want it.
Moreover, eating is instinctive, but not the getting of the

food. We have, therefore, to compare an increase due to an instinctive desire with an increase due to labour. Malthus then admits the difficulty of determining the relationship with exactness; but, " with the natural liking of a Cambridge man for a mathematical simile," he says that the one is to the other as an arithmetical is to a geometrical ratio —which is to say, over any given period of time, population increases by multiplication, food only by addition.

Bonar then goes on to show how Malthus finally leaned away from the mathematical statement of his principal thesis, asserting in the end that all forms of life tend to increase in geometical ratio—in the MacVey Napier Supplement to the Encyclopaedia Britannica (1824). But Malthus' statement is not quite as clear as Bonar seems to consider it. Malthus says that human population could easily double every twenty-five years, but, admitting that improvements and extensions in agriculture would add largely to the supply of food—admitting even that Godwin's communism might improve matters—additions to the food supply would be gained at a constantly increasing expenditure of human effort. Inequalities in the distribution of wealth furthermore can check the efficacy of an increasing food supply quite as definitely as though that increase were lacking. The main point however is the diminishing productiveness of effort applied to the production of food. Summing up, he says, " It follows necessarily that the average rate of the actual increase of population over the greatest part of the globe, obeying the same law as the increase of food, must be totally of a different character from the rate at which it would increase if unchecked."

According then to his one great interpreter, James Bonar —and according to all of his discerning disciples—Malthus makes the actual increase of population depend upon the difficulty (or ease) of getting food.

A curious turn of mind on the part of Malthus is brought out by a quantitative analysis of the Sixth Edition. Two hundred and fifty-three pages are devoted to the " checks to population "—which seemed to enthrall Malthus—whereas he requires only seven pages in which to develop his main thesis, as it is read today and as Wallace and Darwin appropriated it in developing the evolutionary hypothesis of biologic progress.

Properly understood, the Malthus essay then is not an essay on population but an essay on poverty. The author does not explain the cause and manner of population growth; but he does establish convincingly the chief cause of poverty and misery. The central thesis of his essay is not that population increases in geometrical ratio while food increases in arithmetical ratio : Its central thesis is that *life everywhere and always tends to " increase beyond the nourishment prepared for it."* Or, speaking of human beings, " Population has this constant tendency to increase *beyond* the means of subsistence."

CHAPTER III

Critics of Malthus

THE Malthusian controversy was opened of course by Godwin, and therefore became hopelessly entangled at the outset with the idea of the perfectibility of mankind. Godwin was also Malthus' first critic. Common opinion seems to be that Godwin either "disdained to reply" to Malthus or attacked him with classic vulgarity such as Bishop Samuel ("Soapy Sam") Wilberforce brought to bear in his memorable debate with Huxley, when he asked: "Was it through his grandfather or his grandmother that he (Huxley) claimed his descent from a monkey?"[1] To the contrary, Godwin says in his *Thoughts on Dr. Parr's Spital Sermon* (1801), speaking of Malthus,

He has neither laboured to excite hatred nor contempt against me and my tenets; he has argued the question between us just as if they had never been made a theme for political party and the intrigues of faction; he has argued just as if he had no end in view but the investigation of evidence and the development of truth; he has made as unquestionable an addition to the theory of political economy as any writer for a century past. The grand propositions and outlines of his work will, I believe, be found not less conclusive and certain than they are now. For myself I cannot refuse to take some pride in so far as by my writings I gave the occasion and furnished an incentive to the producing of so valuable a treatise.

[1] Huxley, Leonard, *Life and Letters of Thomas Henry Huxley*, New York, 1900.

40

Then, having acknowledged the power and courtesy of his foe, Godwin, advances lustily to attack.

Godwin's attack centers upon the " checks " to population growth—merely, however, the checks of the first essay. Are all schemes for the bettering of mankind foredoomed? Can governments do nothing to prevent the evils of over-population but engage in war; and must they view with entire complacency vice, misery and the fear of premature death? No, Malthus has overlooked much. Godwin then suggests as a corrective the very check upon which Malthus placed greatest stress in later editions of his thesis; for he says that in a state of universal improvement, prudence and pride would prevent too early marriage and overlarge families.

Replying to this attack Malthus ensnares Godwin neatly. He argues that the prudence suggested by Godwin would mean that every man's eye would be open to the main chance. Many persons would therefore secure more than their just share of the material good things of life; and if Godwin attempted to prevent this in his perfect system of life, he would either destroy freedom or disturb the distribution of wealth. Moreover, prudence would prevent a maximum population, and yet Godwin objects to Malthus' idea of limiting numbers; Godwin objects even to the " presence " of society on the ground that it prevents the " greatest practicable population ". Behold Godwin trapped.

In later editions however Malthus made great point of " prudence ", and it is quite probable that this late emphasis may properly be credited to Godwin. Shelley, who was Godwin's son-in-law, says in a footnote of his preface to the *The Revolt of Islam* (1817),

It is remarkable, as a symptom of the revival of public hope, that Malthus has assigned, in the later editions of his work, an indefinite dominion to moral restraint over the principle of

population. This concession answers all the inferences from
his doctrine unfavourable to human improvement, and reduces
the *Essay on Population* to a commentary illustrative of the
unanswerableness of *Political Justice.*

Shelley also says, " Godwin's answer to Malthus is vic-
torious and decisive."   But not quite the perfect son-in-law,
he sums up the " answer " by calling it, " a dry and clever
book, with decent interspersions of cant and sophistry."
The " answer " was contained in Godwin's *Of Population,*
an intolerant, inaccurate, discourteous piece of work, bol-
stered up by a liberal use of scriptural texts.   It is the book
of which William Hazlitt complained in a letter to Leigh
Hunt (21 April, 1821), " I wrote a book in defence of Godwin some years ago, one-half of which he has since stolen
without acknowledgement, without even mentioning my
name, and yet he comes to me to review the very work. . . ."
At first, in arguing against his father and in the 1798
essay, Malthus held that the tendency of numbers to press
upon the food supply—over-propagation—was an immov-
able bar to progress, later he sees it in merely an obstacle
that must be overcome.   Godwin at first considered over-
propagation imaginary, but revealed by subsequent statements (in the *Thoughts*) that he had converted himself to
the later Malthusian views.

In the Godwin-Malthus exchange of broadsides there is
no question—no more than in the Wilberforce-Huxley debate—who emerged victor.   Every school boy or girl has
heard of Huxley: few persons know the name Wilberforce.
Time has declared for Malthus.   In the words of Bonar,
" Malthus has survived his refutation, and Godwin his
reputation."

In 1807, a Puritan or Convenanting pamphlet was thrown
at Malthus.   It was entitled: " A summons of Wakening,
or the evil tendency and danger of speculative Philosophy,

exemplified in Mr. (Sir John) Leslie's *Enquiry into the Nature of Heat,* and Mr. Malthus' *Essay on Population,* and in that speculative system of common law which is at present administered in these kingdoms." The pamphlet proved, to the entire satisfaction of its author, that Malthus was an atheist and guilty of heterodoxy. Our mild country parson however—or his hovering spirit—has become accustomed to this charge. In fact, throughout the nineteenth century, the Malthusian controversy was given a deeply religious and moral flavor, which it has never quite lost. To charge that the author of the essays was an atheist, or irreligious, or even that he did not believe in the perfectability of mankind, carried to the minds of many as clear conviction of error as would scientific proof—just as in this second quarter of the twentieth century a troublesome opponent may often be disposed of merely by calling him a bolshevist.

Possibly the most insupportable of critics is he who, pointing to a magnificent bit of simplicity in which magnificence and simplicity are so intimately interwoven that both appear to the discerning but dual terms applied to one quality, sees in it, "a mere truism." The man of radiant mind must often feel more than cynically inclined when, after stating a compelling truth so clearly that even the dullest may understand, he is faced with the reply that what he has said has always been true and that he has done nothing more than point it out. Has any discoverer, any scientist, or any philosopher done more than point out obvious truth—entirely obvious thereafter, but, to the moment of discovery, as completely obscured to the commonalty of men as the inner surfaces of their own skulls?

Early critics of Malthus were various: the company included economists, parsons, statesmen, lampoonists, philosophers and poets. Coleridge has a great deal to say, some of it slightly indelicate, some of it downright coarse—all contained in the marginalia to his own copy of the second (1803) edition of Malthus' essay, which is in the British museum. " Are we now to have a quarto to teach us that misery and great vice arise from poverty, and that there must be poverty in its worse shape wherever there are more mouths than loaves and more Heads than Brains ! " Here perhaps is the bitter portion of all who write clearly: what they say is too simple, it cannot be significant. So was the great Coleridge minded—and so, too, Hazlitt, who after reading Malthus, " did not see what there was to be proved." An interesting sidelight upon the Coleridgean apostils is given by Bonar:

From some of the phrases dropped in the course of these comments, we should infer they were the preparation for a formal review of the book by Coleridge himself. It is therefore extremely puzzling to find the comments printed almost word for word and letter for letter in a review hitherto considered by every one (Southey included) to be Southey's.

The Coleridgean opinion is summed up in three exclamations: " A philosophical work can have no legitimate purpose but proof and illustration, and three hundred and fifty pages to prove an axiom!—to illustrate a self-evident truth! It is neither more or less than bookmaking ! " In another place Coleridge says of the Malthusian principle: " I solemnly declare that I do not believe that all the heresies and sects, and factions, which the ignorance, and the weakness, and the wickedness of man have ever given birth to, were altogether so disgraceful to man as a Christian, a philosopher, a statesman or citizen, as this abominable tenet." [1]

James Graham in his *An Inquiry into the Principles of Population, Etc.,* (1816) and John Weyland Jr., F. R. S. furnish some interesting though ignorant views of the

---

[1] *Edinburgh Review*, vol. 67, p. 473 n. (January, 1837).

Malthusian essay. According to Graham, Malthus believes famine to be nature's benevolent remedy for the want of food. He finds that Malthus believes nature teaches men to invent diseases to keep population in bounds, finds that Malthus views vice and misery generally as benevolent corrective for over-population and feels that they are to be encouraged rather than suppressed. This is typical of the bulk of the criticism made during Malthus' lifetime.

Empson, in the Edinburgh Review for January 1837, arranges the critics of Malthus who had appeared up to that time in four groups: the purely stupid; " Among these Mr. Graham entitled himself to a distinguished place: " the sentimentally horrified, (Southey, Coleridge and Bishop Huntingford); empiricists, who believe the law of population varies with circumstances, (Godwin, Price, Muret); those who invent laws of their own, (Anderson, Owen and Poulett Scrope); then he puts Weyland in a special group by himself made up of the inordinately obdurate who deny the premises of Malthus as well as his conclusions.

Weyland, in his *Principles of Population and Production* (1816), says that " Population has a natural tendency to keep *within* [2] the powers of the soil to afford it subsistence in every graduation through which society passes," (which is to say) " that every man has a natural tendency to remain in prison who is necessarily confined to it by four strong walls." Malthus replies pertinently that we could as soon infer that the pines of the crowded Norwegian forest have no tendency to send out lateral branches, but as every knows, a Norwegian pine standing in an open place sends out superb sweeping boughs from apex to butt. Finally Weyland, like so many critics of Malthus, runs directly into the great essayist's camp; he declares that with first-rate farming and a

[1] *Edinburgh Review*, vol. 67, p. 491.

[2] Italics, ours.

well-developed division of labor, country people might be
enabled to move up to the city, and, by their unhealthy manner of life in the towns, die off at a rate that would prevent
population from pressing upon the food supply.

In refuting Weyland, Malthus puts forward a proposition
much like the formula submitted and developed in the
present work: " Population invariably increases where the
means of subsistence increases, *unless prevented by some
very powerful and obvious checks.*" [1]   Chapters, in which the
central thesis of the present work are developed suggest as
the " *powerful and obvious checks* " those set to work by the
desire for higher standards of living.

In 1830, M. T. Sadler, M. P., after asserting that Malthus'
ideas were so " horrible " as to have " no parallel in moral
literature, sacred or profane," pronounces a " law of population " to the effect that " the prolificness of human beings,
otherwise similarly circumstanced, varies inversely as their
numbers." [2]   Ten years later Archibald Alison delivered
himself of twin volumes devoted to expanding the proposition that population increases inversely with density.[3]   The
following decade brought a third formal offer of a " true "
law of population: Thomas Doubleday asserted that population increases inversely with the supply of aliment.[4]

No anthology of early Malthusian critics is properly composed if it does not include the irrepressible Practical Man.
Arthur Young fills this rôle.   Ignorance rushes in where
Erudition dares not venture.   He denies the axiom that
what cannot be ought not to be, and feels very strongly that
when a man marries without means, he may justly blame
society if it does not provide for his family.   In his earlier
writings however Young takes the Malthusian view:

[1] *Essay on Population*, 7th ed., I, ii, p. 12n and 2nd ed., p. 16.
[2] Sadler, M. T., *The Law of Population*, London, 1830, p. 368.
[3] Alison, A., *Principles of Population*, London, 1840, vol. ii, p. 465.
[4] *True Law of Population*, London, 1853, pp. 5 and 20.

There are in England many marriages and much bastardy among the poor, owing to our poor laws, which add no useful population whatever to the state; for to have those born who, if they live, must be maintained by the industry of others, is about as valuable a population as a standing army, with this only difference, that they may not be altogether so perniciously employed. Hence therefore it is the amount of industry that should be attended to, rather than the population. If the former declines, the increase of the latter, supposing it generally possible, would be mischievous to national prosperity, and rather prove the misery than the happiness of a country.[1]

So much for pre-Darwinian critics of Malthus.

Thoughtful socialists of course deny Malthus, though a few of them are pliable enough to include neo-Malthusianism in their schemes. Whether neo-Malthusianism and Malthusianism are the same thing, or mutually exclusive, is however not quite clear. Fortunately that need not be settled here. This much however is plain: Orthodox Socialism and the unadorned first proposition of Malthus are irreconcilable. If mankind, in the way of all other kinds, presses constantly against the barriers of life to his own destruction, mere padding or cushioning of barriers, or even expanding their scope, by socialism or any other -ism would be of no— or, at best, of temporary—effect. How could Marx speak otherwise than:

New machinery is constantly supplanting labour without any real compensation in increasing demand, either at once or in the long run. The fund from which wages are paid increases less rapidly than machinery. This can result only in the progressive production of a population which, in relation to capital is a surplus or superfluity, an over-population: the cause which increases the net revenue of the country at the same time

[1] *Annals of Agric.*, vol. ii, Review of New Publications relating to Agriculture, pp. 420-21, ed. 1784.

renders the population redundant and deteriorates the condition of the labourer. So far from deploring the existence of this redundant class, the capitalists depend on it, as the reserve of their army.[1]

The Socialist's dilemma is that he must demonstrate the misery and helplessness of labour and at the same time show that it is due to the machinery of capitalism—and not to one of the most avid of innate tendencies, over-propagation.

Henry George, an American of engaging intellect and a rare power of words, points his pen very definitely at Malthus in his *Progress and Poverty*. He does not however offer new criticism, in fact, it is all to be found in Godwin and Sadler. Excessive numbers, according to George, are not the result of bad calculation on the part of Providence; they are the result of bad institutions and faulty government. Malthus, in Henry George's opinion, gets wound up in his idea of a madly increasing population and loses sight of actual increase, which falls far short of world limitations.[2] Then a devastating bit of logic: Had there been such a law as Malthus', it would have been sooner recognized! Furthermore an increase of population brings an increase in food, since the division of labour enables man to produce more than he consumes, and we find that the most populous countries are the most wealthy. Here George is right to the extent that a division of labor speeds up wealth production—as do many other devices—but man's powers of proliferation and his cupidity outrun all bounds. Man produces wealth and reproduces his kind; but human beings and especially their wants multiply through processes far more facile than those by which wealth is created.

[1] These words are put into the mouth of Marx by Bonar, but they form a fair summary of the Marxian population attitude. (See *Malthus and His Work*, pp. 388-89.)

[2] George, H., *Progress and Poverty*, New York, 1899, p. 94.

At least one observation of Henry George's however cannot be disposed of lightly; he maintains that population growth tends to subside with the advent of higher living-standards. Malthus, he says, does not see that the slowness of population growth results, in part, because " there is a third check which comes into play with the elevation of the standard of comfort." Here is the second clause—or something very like the second clause—of the hypothesis to which this book is devoted. Here also George, by recognizing the necessity for checks to population growth, goes over into Malthus' camp.

George next quotes the venerable adage, " a rich man for luck and a poor man for children," and substantiates it by citing Adam Smith's " not uncommon . . . half-starved Highland woman . . . the mother of twenty-three or twenty-four children." He then sets forth what he considers to be the real law of population growth:

The tendency to increase, instead of being always uniform, is strong where a greater population would give increased comfort and where the perpetuity of the race is threatened by the mortality induced by adverse conditions, but weakens just as the higher development of the individual becomes possible, and the perpetuity of the race is assured.[1]

Orthodox economists from Ricardo to Jevons accepted Malthus to the last comma. Population theories advanced by later economists differed from the Malthusian view. They had, moreover, so much in common that their authors may be considered a school of population theorists—the Optimists. These men, writing on the turn of the twentieth century, thought Malthus substantially right in and for his day, but that a rising tide of new wealth had submerged his principle. Industrialism had everywhere triumphed. Ma-

[1] George, H., *Progress and Poverty*, New York, 1899, p. 138.

chinery and the playthings of the new century had so far ameliorated the life of man that the burden of the struggle for existence was scarcely felt—or its burden had been entirely shaken off.   Let us call these witnesses.

Professor Patten, of the University of Pennsylvania, saw in the industrial life of his day and hour an entirely new basis for civilization.[1]   He sounded full blast the optimistic note that heralded the new century in America.   That note was not so provincial however as many esoteric auditors have felt; for it reverberated, with varying degrees of distinctness, throughout the work of Professor Marshall in England, Professor Cassell in Sweden, Doctor Pierson in Holland, Professor Levasseur in France and Signor Nitti in Italy.   In fact it was everywhere the *fin de siecle,* or turn-of-the-century, view:

The standard of living rose; the cost of living continued to fall, and man's conquest over nature seemed well-nigh complete. Then it was that, in spite of the warning voices of Mill and Jevons, the progress of the human race towards material and spiritual perfection was generally believed, in Western Europe, to be continuous and inevitable.   Malthus, with his *Principles of Population,* and Ricardo, with his Law of Diminishing Returns were discredited.[2]

These lines from Professor Wright of Cambridge suggest an international diapason with which the American scholars were certainly not entirely out of harmony.

Professor R. T. Ely, another American economist, finds that population increases wherever an increase in wealth affords opportunity, but it does not follow that the Malthusian theory is, in strict interpretation, true; population has not increased as rapidly as wealth.   What does Professor

[1] Patten, S. N., *The New Basis of Civilization*, New York, 1907, p. 16.
[2] Wright, H., *Population*, New York, 1923, pp. 166-167.

Ely mean by this? He hints, certainly, that capitalism and industrialism have brought a machine-made heaven. But a little further on Professor Ely writes an extremely significant sentence, pointing toward the fact that there is a direct relationship between population and wealth, and an inverse relationship between population and living-standards: the formula set down in our first chapter.

If there had been no increase in population during the last one hundred and fifty years, the marginal productivity of labor would (if, nevertheless, modern methods of production had been developed) have been very much higher than it is, and wages would have been correspondingly higher than they are.[1]

Professor F. W. Taussig of Harvard after making what seems an over-statement of the Malthusian principle, manages to create an appearance of having discredited it. But on a later page he comes nearer than any of his American colleagues to an acceptance of the Malthusian formula. He is alarmed to find birth control, which operates first among the more cultured classes, producing a dysgenic trend in the birth rate, with consequent deterioration of populations. Finally Taussig takes a position facing directly toward our own formula: he thinks that the gradual spread of birth control will bring population growth so completely under command that poverty, misery and vice will tend to disappear.[2]

Points at which the population theories of Professor Taussig and his American colleagues fail to coincide are of no great significance. Patten, Ely, Taussig, Seligman and other leaders in the most recent school of American economists all held that the machinery of modern civilization had

[1] Ely, R. T., *Outlines of Economics*, 3rd ed., New York, 1908, p. 436.

[2] Taussig, F. W., *Principles of Economics*, edition of 1911, vol. ii, pp. 220-225.

carried man to a plane slightly above the working of the Malthusian principle.

What is the view of the late dean of British economists? Modern machinery has released mankind from the yoke and burden of the Malthusian principle:

We have already noticed [says Alfred Marshall] that the English economists of the earlier half of the nineteenth century over-rated the tendency of an increasing population to press upon the means of subsistence; and it was not Malthus' fault that he could not foresee the great development of steam transport by land and by sea, which have enabled Englishmen of the present generation to obtain the products of the richest lands of the earth at a comparatively small cost.

Here Marsnall stands shoulder to shoulder with the earliest twentieth century school of American economists. But then Marshall takes water on the other shoulder—much as Taussig did, with this difference: Taussig thought the Malthusian principle operated only upon persons who were on the starvation margin and not upon more fortunately situated groups, while Marshall felt that the principle applied only to backward nations and that nations of western civilization were exempt. As western standards of material comfort flow outward to the economically backward nations of the earth the populations of these nations must decline in numbers, or rather, if their populations go on increasing they can never hope to attain the living standards of Western Europe.[1] Marshall's language is slightly indefinite, but by clear implication he here suggests the second clause of our hypothesis: population and living-standards tend to maintain an inverse relationship.

The opinion that science, technology and business efficiency may raise mankind above the reach of the iron claw

[1] Marshall, Alfred, *Principles of Economics* (sixth edition, London, 1910), pp. 178-180; third edition, London, 1895, p. 259.

of natural selection—or of the Malthusian principle—a view
that may be called the turn-of-the-twentieth-century view,
had its prophet in the writer of a news article to which William Hazlitt made vigorous reply.   Writing in 1828 Hazlitt
said,

It was stated the other day in the papers that the effect that
might result to the community, and to civilization in general,
from Mr. Gurney's new invention of a steam-carriage to run
on common roads, were incalculable, alluding to the immense
number of horses now kept for stage coaches, and the saving
of all the expense, or turning it into a different channel for the
support and growth of food for human beings.   If so much
benefit can be done to society by a single invention, in leaving
so much disposable food for human population, who shall say
what good cannot be done by other inventions or discoveries.
But at any rate it must be granted by the persons so arguing,
that this portion of subsistence has been artificially drawn off
from the support of the mass of the community, to pamper the
pride and pleasure of the idle or the wealthy in riding in stage
coaches.   The load that has been laid on the produce and
industry of the country will now, it is said, be taken off by one
man's ingenuity and science.

Having slain the false prophet, Hazlitt pins this note upon
his husk: " Those who run their heads against Mr. Malthus'
general doctrine, that population may increase faster than
and beyond the means of subsistence, only run their heads
against a post."   Then, still speaking of Malthus, Hazlitt
places upon his work an estimate much like the one included
in our third chapter: " All that can be done is to deny his
sovereign right over this doctrine as the inventor and legis-
lator of it, to show his illogicality and inconsistence in reasoning upon what was not his own, and his perverse and
partial application of a general and important principle." [1]

[1] Hazlitt, William, *Outlines of Political Economy, New Writings* collected by P. P. Howe (New York, 1927), pp. 198-220.

M. Levasseur, arch-optimist among French *fin-de-siecle* economists, was, like Marshall and the Americans, far from sound on the gospel according to British nineteenth century saints of political economy. The magic of machinery and electricity convinced M. Levasseur that the law of dominishing returns should be re-examined; quite possibly machinery and electricity had made it obsolete. Science, with its new chemistry, its aluminum, its promised harnessing of the tides assured a good living to the human kind for an indefinite period. This venerable French sage writes in the purest strain of the McKinley period of American economic philosophy.[1] (Possibly it would be better to say, merely, the American strain of economic philosophy. For, beginning with Carey, there were always prominent economists in the flourishing young republic who were eager to deny the law of diminishing—anything.)

Professor Gustave Cassel of the University of Stockholm has managed to write a book on economics—*Social Economy,* he calls it—with scarcely a word on the problem of population and without a single reference to Malthus. So eminent an economist cannot be omitted however from a survey of pre-war population theories. Professor Cassel appears to revert to the ancient Mercantilist doctrine that in numbers there is wealth, that production is dependent upon the growth of population, and not population upon the growth of wealth. But later, in discussing Ricardo's theory of rent and the iron law of wages, he indicates a considerable if not complete sympathy with the Malthusian proposition.[2]

The optimism of F. S. Nitti, Italian economist and states-

[1] Levasseur, P. E., *La Population Française*, Paris, 1889-1892, vol. iii, chapter ii.

[2] Cassel, G., *The Theory of Social Economy*, London, 1923, vol. i, pp. 34, 35 and 213.

man, is temperate; it is in fact very much in the Cassel or
Adam Smith strain. Briefly, the production of human
beings always proportions itself to the production of the
means of subsistence. Signor Nitti also has great faith in
the democratization of distribution, the internationalization
of markets, and a natural diminution of human fecundity,
as influences tending to offset the pressure of population
upon the means of subsistence. Though not an ebullient
Godwinite, Nitti is quite obviously an anti-Malthusian.[1]

Professor Gide, best known among very early twentieth
century French economists, believed as Nitti (and Spencer,
from whom perhaps they both derived their idea) that civilization brings with it decreased fecundity, an actual biologic
change in the human organism, which should in time refute
Malthus.[2] Possibly it is this biologic twist that distin-
guishes European optimists most clearly from their American contemporaries, who based their high hopes upon purely
economic considerations.

The Dutch economist, Doctor N. G. Pierson, presents a
thorough-going discussion of population, but he is incon-
clusive. Among pre-war economists he most nearly approaches an unequivocal neo-Malthusianism—if we except
Leroy-Beaulieu with whom Doctor Pierson however takes
issue. He acknowledges the grain of truth contained in
Leroy-Beaulieu's assertions and maintains that if the standard of living of the working classes could be raised to the
level of the well-to-do, early marriages, and consequently
the number of births, would decline. But this decline is
itself a condition precedent to social improvement. There
is little evidence therefore that the standard-of-living check

[1] Nitti, F. S., *Population and the Social System*, London, 1894, chapters
2 and 3.

[2] Gide, C. S., *Principles of Political Economy* (translation), Boston,
1891, pp. 320-323.

will ever apply to the increase of the working classes.
Further on, Doctor Pierson takes over without reservation
the doctrine of birth control:

What then remains?   Nothing, except the moral restraint
preached by Malthus himself, and the so-called Neo-Malthusianism advocated by some of his followers of the present day.
There is no third way.   But who believes that moral restraint
will ever be widely practised?   The force, which draws the
sexes together, and does not spring from the baser passions
alone, is generally so strong that no exhortation, however
solemnly delivered, can prevail against it.   To forgo the pleas-
ures of marriage, simply because marriage involves the risk of
falling to a lower rung of the social ladder demands a degree
of civilization which the majority have not yet attained.   The
same thing cannot be said of neo-Malthusianism.   It preaches
no celibacy and makes no demand—at least no heavy demand—
on self-restraint.   Its advantages can be understood by the
most ignorant, for it stops that increase in the number of the
family which mars the happiness of many married couples.[1]

Very shrewdly Doctor Pierson and most of his European
colleagues link population and production as sub-topics in
one general discussion, indicating it seems, appreciable adherence to the broad outlines of the formula: populations
tend to increase directly with wealth and inversely with the
standard of living—as the following summary sentences
from Pierson go to show:—

Moral restraint and neo-Malthusianism—our choice lies between
these two so long as we are in search of means for checking the
growth of the population.   But the question on which we are
now engaged has to do not only with growth of the population,
but with population and production.   The average income must
be raised, and there are two ways in which this may be affected;

[1] Pierson, N. G., *Principles of Economics*, New York, 1912, p. 165.

the one consists in what we have set forth (voluntary parent-hood) the other in increasing the volume of production.

Do any of these men submit a complete theory of population growth? They are all content with attacking Malthus, or they present population theories which upon close examination turn out to be explanations of poverty—or of well-being—and not explanations of the mode of human increase. For that matter, it may be recalled that the essential and surviving idea contained in Malthus' essay explains the universality of poverty rather than the growth of populations. But it is not quite fair to say that Malthus did not at least attempt a complete theory of population growth: he said that food tends to increase in arithmetic ratio and population in geometric ratio: that was a theory of population growth—but a wrong one. None of the " Optimists " however even attempts an explanation of the mode of human increase. That, no orthodox economist has essayed—since Malthus.

CHAPTER IV

EAST AND PEARL

FOLLOWING the World War, interest in population problems increased. Several excellent works appeared in Western Europe and in the United States. Two of the most significant came, curiously enough, from American biologists—curiously enough because no first-rate biologist has heretofore grappled with the population problem; and again, because America was for a century preceding the World War considered the one nation of Western civilization that had no population problem. Professor Raymond Pearl's book on *The Biology of Population Growth* is an excellent example of the power and limitation of an almost purely statistical treatment of biological and social problems. Professor Pearl is primarily a biologist, but a facile statistician as well. Professor E. M. East's *Mankind at the Crossroads* is second to none among twentieth-century works on the problem of population. Unlike Pearl, he uses the philosophical and historical methods with only a casual employment of the statistical method or even of statistics.

The problem presented by population growth is at bottom biologic—what could be more obvious? Secondly, it is an economic problem. Finally it is a psychologic problem. In a later chapter it will appear that in this modern day it is the tertiary, psychologic factor that controls population growth, because birth rates are determined by psycho-economic considerations—and because economics is largely psychology.

Since human increase is fundamentally a biologic matter

58

it is gratifying therefore—if surprising—to find two eminent, professing biologists, Pearl and East, volunteering to
lay the foundation for a twentieth-century reconsideration
of the population problem.

What do these men, writing on the eve of the second
quarter of the current century, tell us of population growth?
Very appropriately, East rests his case upon the simple prem-
ise that man is an animal, a highly cerebrated animal it is
true, but still an animal. In considering any human problem
it is a mistake, he thinks, to neglect the biologic viewpoint;
it is essential to any sane treatment of the problem of population. In a voice that will be heard again in the next
chapter (coming from Mr. Swinburne) East then empha-
sizes the hopeless relativity of all economic progress.

Professor East is probably the most completely orthodox
Malthusian that has put pen to paper with any significant
result. In fact he exceeds Malthus: not only does he see
in food the ultimate check to population growth, but it
seems to loom up before him as a nearby or immediate
check. The vacant spaces of the earth are filling fast, and
the utmost yield is needed from each unit of arable land.
Moreover, when the land is filled, human nature will not
have changed. The conflict to survive may be sublimated
to an extent; but innate eagerness to survive at all costs
will remain an elemental character of the human protoplasm,
ready to show itself when sufficiently stimulated — and it
will be stimulated more and more frequently as the struggle
becomes keener. At the worst, it will provoke catastrophes
like the recent World War; at best there will be economic
strife, with physical results less catastrophic perhaps but
fully as deadly.[1]

When it comes to remedies, East differs from Malthus.

[1] East, E. M., *Mankind at the Crossroads* (Charles Scribner's Sons,
1923), pp. 343-344.

He is the out-and-out birth control advocate—though it is perhaps not unfair to assume that Malthus would have entertained similar views had not his mind been held in the religious and traditional clamps of his age. Even in the present enlightened — or perhaps merely advanced—era, it is hard to imagine one who has willingly accepted religious orders, and who is a teacher in a company-owned college, advocating radical views of any sort: to compass fairly Malthus' view one must read behind his lines.

East's position, however, is manifest. The only possible relief from overpopulation is to call a halt on population growth at a point long before the subsistence limit is reached, at a point where there is no intense struggle for mere existence. The obvious means of accomplishing this feat is the conscious, deliberate control of "fecundity." [1] To endeavor to raise more food would bring at best only temporary relief. An increasing population would take up all slack. In final case the world can support but so many persons. The vessel is elastic, it is true, but it is a closed vessel nevertheless. Enhanced efficiency and prudent conservation can bring increased happiness only if numbers remain constant.

According to Professor East food supplies control the growth of populations. He warns that mankind will soon proliferate far beyond the power of all available means to sustain his numbers. Overpopulation and consequent disaster are at hand. But ought we not to remind this biologist that *there has always been overpopulation*—if he will permit us to except comparatively small regions and brief reaches of time? By what curious laboratory-engendered amnesia do first-rate scientists lose sight of the first axiom of biology: *life tends everywhere and always to exceed the warrant for it?*

[1] East says *fecundity*, but he undoubtedly means the *birth rate*.

Let us hasten past what Professor East says of " over-populated regions " in temperate Asia and the major part of Europe, the " over-populated regions " of the western hemisphere, of Africa and of Australia, until we reach what appears to be the core of his thesis:

Growth can be maintained only at a rate which parallels the enhancement of crop yields through plant breeding, pest-control, and scientific agronomy, a snail-like progress at best. Those who cherish the hope of a sudden extension of the allowance Mother Nature grants her children when this time comes are likely to be disappointed. There is no indication either in physics, chemistry, or the natural sciences of agriculture being able to profit by such radical changes as have occurred in mechanics. . . . We raise more wheat to feed more men to raise more wheat to feed more men.[1]

Have we not quoted fully enough from Professor East's earnest and painstaking work to leave no doubt about his trend of reasoning? Is it not clear that he believes population growth to be controlled by food supplies? In some mysterious way, however, populations have in the past (hundreds of thousands of generations, be it remembered) kept workably within bounds; it is only today, or in our grandchildren's generation that population growth will bump disastrously, perhaps fatally, into the sustenance limit. By way of final contribution he drops Malthus' old coin into the plate—or Malthus' coin reminted and bearing the awful legend: Population will " some fifty years hence " overflow all bounds and bring undreamed-of misery and disaster.

Professor East's remedy is birth control. He thinks, however, that there is no present evidence of this remedy saving the situation—or any large probability that it will. Curiously enough he nevertheless points out much that agrees precisely with a conclusion reached in our final chapter:

[1] *Op. cit.*, pp. 345-346.

Population will probably become stabilized — possibly at a figure lower than the present world total.[1]

In saying that a declining birth rate will not halt the impasse between population growth and food supply, and then admitting that it has actually halted it " in a very small fraction of the white population," Professor East treads upon what economists have learned is very dangerous ground. He is predicting that an invention, or rather a practice that adds to man's comfort, will remain for long the property of an esoteric few. But in 1900 " wireless " was to remain an ingenious toy, automobiles would be mere playthings for the rich. (Twenty years earlier, it appeared that telephone and incandescent light were in the same categories.) Annually, since 1908, puzzled economists have been predicting an imminent saturation point in the use of automobiles. The human animal may be a little dull about ideals, but anything that betters his physical ease becomes general with almost scandalous rapidity.

So long as world economy was almost wholly and uniformly agricultural, the crux of the population problem was the ratio between the number of persons living upon a square mile of land and the amount of food that square mile produced—or could be made to produce.

Then machinery, the machinery of manufacture and the machinery of transportation, came into use; man created utilities and values other than food; he exchanged those values for food brought to his door by new and constantly improved means of transportation: the population problem then became a matter of the ratio between *wealth* produced in a given area—whether of food or of products that could be exchanged for food—and the number of people living in that area. Rapidly man accustomed himself to the satisfying of wants beyond mere hunger. He learned to desire

[1] *Op. cit.*, pp. 344-348.

luxurious shelter, elaborate clothing, swift transportation, easy education, automatic amusement—in brief, the means of gratifying with a minimum effort his mind and spirit as well as his belly. Professor East, a biologist, thinking in terms of esophogus, stomach, jejunum and duodenum— thinking mainly in terms of the alimentary tract—has over-looked the fact that man strives, struggles, and bitterly competes even in this second quarter of the twentieth century, not for food, not for living, but for a way of living.

A further word of comment upon Professor East's ideas: birth control is his remedy for overpopulation, but he fears it will be employed too late to halt oncoming disaster. Professor East, thinking of legislative restrictions upon the dissemination of birth-control information, has lost sight of the fact that provisions even of the federal constitution are not quite rigidly enforced. One may not, in a scientific work, take sides, nor put birth control or other propaganda on the counter. One does not, perhaps, exceed decent caution however in mentioning that there is apparent evidence that birth control is more nearly universal in our Western civilization than the bathtub and the telephone.

Professor East himself points out that the reproductive capacity of the human animal is liberal, that it is represented by a potential *birth rate* of at least sixty per thousand. Nowhere in the Western civilization however, not even among the lowest peasants of remotest Russia, does the *actual birth rate* exceed forty per thousand, and in regions which may be considered in strictest sense part of the Western civilization, birth rates nowhere exceed twenty-five per thousand. This is not conclusive evidence of course of the universality of birth control; but even the most skeptical will probably admit that if deliberate interference with the procreative process is not universal, the wide difference between potential and actual birth rates indicates an extremely widespread practice of contraception or of abstention.

No brief is offered here for the birth-control movement, or for any other movement; the aim is merely to clear the view for persons who pretend to be opposed to any slightest consideration of voluntary parenthood—by calling to their attention that it is not in exclusive suburban areas alone, nor solely among Vassar graduates or Harvard graduates that offspring number less than two per couple. Offsetting each carpenter, plumber or even truck driver, who is the father of four or more children, five other members of his union can be brought forward who have but one, or two, or none.[1] These anti-birth control irreconcilables, it appears, are opposed to the " slightest discussion " of a practice that is general.

.   .   .   .

What Professor Raymond Pearl has to say in the main body of his book is very clear. In summing up, however, he muddies the current by saying:

Long experience with experimental work has taught me that a somewhat rough and ready, but on the whole dependable, rule is that any natural phenomenon which, in advance of observation of the event, can be proved by purely logical processes to be necessarily so, almost invariably turns out upon really competent and penetrating trial or observation to be in fact not so at all but quite otherwise.[2]

This distrust of " pure logical process " is indeed curious. It cannot be that Pearl distrusts the whole method of science; he must mean that he distrusts one sub-process of

[1] This statement is based on an investigation conducted under the writer's direction. When completed, it was found that owing to faulty verbal instructions given to those questioned, the result was questionable. It is therefore not presented in quantitative form, but the evidence leaves little doubt of the general truth of the above statement.

[2] Pearl, R., *The Biology of Population Growth*, Alfred A. Knopf, New York, 1925, pp. 210-211.

the method of science—deduction. Professor Pearl, however, is speaking more heedlessly here than is his wont in condemning so flatly the deductive method which gave the world the first Malthus essay! Furthermore, this first Malthus essay gave to Professor Pearl and all who profess the biological sciences one of their most significant generalizations. Two massive facts command attention: the first Malthus essay was as purely deductive as human thought can be; it struck a light that has illumined the workings of the bio-universe more fully than any other human writing. We cannot discard Professor Pearl's findings on account of his prejudice, however distrustful he may be of all methods of science other than the experimental and statistical subdivisions of induction, for in the use of those two tools he is skilful.

Professor Pearl's principal contentions appear in six catagorical statements:

First, that populations grow in size according to the same mathematical law that individual animals and plants follow in the growth of their bodies in size. Second, that human populations grow in size according to the same law as do the experimental populations of lower organisms and in turn as do individual plants and animals in body size.

In the experiments and observations leading to these conclusions Pearl finds that individual plants and animals, including men, and colonies of living forms of whatever kind, follow a slanting " S-shaped " curve of growth. Does this mean that all growth begins slowly, increases more rapidly and then gradually slows down until a maximum size is reached.[1] Is that conclusion new? Philosophically, it has

[1] This curve is described by the late Sir George Handley Knibbs, professor of Physics at the University of Sidney, Australia: " Initially it is concave upwards; its middle is sensibly linear; after that it becomes convex upwards, and approaches a limiting value asymptotically. That

long been the possession of biologists and of thoughtful persons in general. Since all organisms are cells or mere colonies of cells, more or less specialized and structurally associated, it is not extraordinary that all growth, whether in size or in numbers, is included in one formula. Professor Pearl's important contribution consists in presenting this idea accurately through the use of diagrams and statistical method. He establishes the fact that growth may be represented by a mathematical curve, but he does not go to the point of asserting that his curve may be used as a means of predicting future population growth. He says in fact that his curve of growth may be upset at any point, that in the past it has been broken at many points and displaced this way or that.

Whenever a new form of human economy appears, this curve of Pearl's breaks in two; it is shifted sharply upward or downward—indicating a sharp repression or stimulation of population growth, depending upon whether the new form of economy is more or less productive than the one it supersedes. In sum, Professor Pearl's curve tells us simply that the mode of population growth can be expressed mathematically and illustrated graphically by a smooth curve—but that this curve and its whole meaning can be destroyed at any time by inventions, by discoveries in science and by radical changes in economic, political or social institutions. Since these sudden changes are usually for the better, anti-Malthusians of all sorts (the " optimists," for example) flourish at such times—and later, decline.

Contrary to East's prediction, Pearl says:

Should the somewhat inexorable advance in the number of

is to say, as time goes on the population-numbers increase more and more rapidly, per unit of time; attain to a maximum rate of increase; then increase more and more slowly as the numbers approach the limiting number of the population." *The Shadow of the World's Future*, London, 1928, p. 54.

people on this globe which the biological law of population growth makes extremely probable, lead us to view-with-alarm? It seems to me that if we so conclude, we ought equally to be concerned about the orderly growth of any baby into man- or womanhood. For I am quite firmly convinced that the biological inevitability of the one form of growth is not greater than that of the other.[1]

Here Professor Pearl has apparently overlooked something. He has left, presumably, the familiar field of his own experiments and statistics, and has forgotten for the moment the experimental findings of his colleagues—particularly when he says, " I am quite convinced that the biological inevitability of the one form of growth is no greater than that of the other." Growth of individuals is not " inevitable." Osborn and Mendel have controlled the growth of albino rats almost completely, halting their growth entirely for 268 days, then speeding it up until finally normal size was reached.[2]

Everyone is familiar with the means of controlling growth in human beings: through diet, through exercise, and particularly through undersecretion and oversecretion of the endocrine or ductless glands—or through feeding the product of these glands.

To discover that with undisturbed economic, political and other social circumstances, a given population yields a mathematical curve of growth exactly similar to the mathematical curve of undisturbed individual growth does not explain the mode of human increase. There is but one logical and inescapable conclusion to be drawn from Pearl's analogy: If, as he says, population growth is exactly like individual

[1] *Op. cit.*, p. 210.

[2] Osborn, T. B. and Mendel, L. B., *Feeding Experiments with Isolated Food-Substances*, Carnegie Institution, Washington, 1911; Mendel, L. B., *Nutrition*, Yale University Press, 1923.

growth, population growth is bound to slow down and stop. It is almost incredible that Pearl did not go on to that conclusion.

Since biologists have opened up a vista through which one can see individual size determined at will, it should require no great effort to see population size determined completely and universally in accord with individual and group comfort and aspirations.

Professor Pearl's fourth conclusion would be of very great significance if it could be taken—as it has been taken by many readers—at its face value: " Rate of production or fertility is negatively correlated with density of population." It is difficult to believe, however, that Professor Pearl means us to assume that mere density of population, aside from all implications of scarcity of food, scarcity of air, scarcity of light, difficulty of movement, produces internal biological changes which result in reduced fecundity; for his experiments, though carried out with extreme care, are not reassuring on all of these and some other points. Therefore this fourth conclusion, which has been considered by many students of population growth as Pearl's prime contribution in that field, must be ruled out until it becomes clear that the reduced fertility which Professor Pearl notes does not proceed from any of the suggested—or other—causes.

Furthermore, does not Pearl's formula exceed all probable warrant in suggesting that anything properly called biologic fecundity, undisturbed by purely mechanical or chemical effects, could be controlled by the extent of space (or volume) occupied by a colony of this or that life form. A philosopher or an economist might be expected to handle carelessly the terms *fertility* and *fecundity,* but to see biologists pass lightly over these points is bitterly discouraging. Birth rates can be tampered with; in fact, controlled as definitely as the flow of water from a tap; but a careful survey of the literature of biology reveals nowhere a flat-out statement by a reliable biologist that fecundity is *in general* controlled by anything beside the age-long flow of time and circumstance.

Curiously enough this formula of Pearl's was advanced by Sadler just a century ago.[1] Sadler said, " The prolificness of human beings, otherwise similarly circumstanced, varies inversely as their numbers." The concluding comment of the *Edinburgh Review* for July, 1839 upon this formula is interesting: " We have shown that Mr. Sadler is careless in the collection of facts, [and] that he is incapable of reasoning on facts when he has collected them." [2]

Sir George Handley Knibbs, First Commonwealth Statistician, Australia, says of Pearl's formula: " The plausibility of this view is such that it cannot be passed without comment." His subsequent criticism of the Pearl formula is not quite complete, but it is destructive.[3]

Unlike reproductive capacity, birth rates are extremely variable. One can therefore lend a ready ear to Professor Pearl's fifth finding:

that [the] birth rate is negatively correlated with wealth (or positively correlated with poverty), and that the differential birth rate on this economic base constitutes one of the menacing features of human population growth, which, however, can possibly be met in some part by an entirely free dissemination of knowledge about birth control.[4]

Pearl's sixth and last finding is " that the indirect psychological and social effects of relative poverty as contrasted

[1] Sadler, M. T., *The Law of Population*, London, 1830.

[2] *Edinburgh Review*, vol. 51, p. 321.

[3] Knibbs, Sir George H., *The Shadow of the World's Future*, London, 1928, pp. 54-55.

[4] *Op. cit.*, p. 209.

with relative wealth express themselves definitely and clearly in the sexual activity of human beings, and through sexual activity to birth rates." [1]   But how can there be any significant correlation between the frequency of what Professor Pearl rightly implies is a form of domestic diversion, or recreation, and the actual birth rate?   Pearl himself says that, in a random group, frequency of coition will vary from less than once a month to more than sixty times a month. It is only necessary to recall that frequency of child birth cannot not exceed by much one in twelve months, and, on the average, does not exceed one in one hundred months, during the entire child-bearing period, to see the futility of attributing variations in birth rates to slight, general variations in frequency of coition.

A final salute is owing nevertheless to Professor Pearl for his persistent adherence to the statistical method.   The prerogative of final judgment upon the problem of population, and upon the validity of the hypothesis offered in this book, must be reserved of course for the statistician.   At present, however, the data of population are neither full enough nor accurate enough to warrant a thoroughly statistical treatment of population problems. [2]

Though East and Pearl stand out in a remarkable way from twentieth-century theorizers upon the growth of populations, Professor Carr-Saunders' book is, in the opinion of many students, the most scholarly in that field of interest. It is reasonable, however, that the theories of these two American biologists should be examined together, and that the work of Carr-Saunders and several less complete or slightly less compelling post-war theories of population growth should be discussed in the next chapter.

[1]   *Op. cit.*, p. 209.

[2]   Bowley, A. L., "Some Tests of the Trustworthiness of Public Statistics," *Economica*, December, 1928.

CHAPTER V

OTHER POST-WAR THEORIES

WAR and its aftermath—especially unemployment, which in 1920 and 1921 was acute nearly everywhere—should have produced in Europe a broad and penetrating literature of population, but it did not. In England, where almost a million and a half persons were out of employment during the entire decade immediately following the armistice; in Germany and in Italy, where unemployment was less acute but where it was complicated by unaccustomed political arrangements, not one painstaking and coherent pronouncement upon the subject of population appeared—if we except Carr-Saunders' excellent work.[1]

In America an incredible prosperity soon distracted attention from every other concern. But in spite of the almost complete relief from population pressure afforded by prosperity there is a keener interest in population problems in the United States than elsewhere, though in every quarter of the globe population pressure is coming to be recognized as the chief cause of nearly all varieties of friction and distress in human affairs.

Doctor J. S. Sweeney is Professor Pearl's pupil, and it is fair to assume that everything he writes is simply an extension or revision of the Pearl idea. Doctor Sweeney introduces a "vital index": ($100 B/D$), one hundred times the birth rate divided by the death rate. He explains that this measure indicates "the biological soundness of a population in so far as its survival in existent conditions is concerned."

[1] Carr-Saunders, A. M., *The Population Problem*, Oxford, 1922.

Applying this measure to various national and regional groups, Doctor Sweeney adds the weight of reliable statistical evidence to opinion already widely established among population experts, that countries occupying equatorial areas produce " smaller mean indices " than countries lying further away from the equator: in equatorial regions, terrific birth rates are more than offset by devastating death rates. Sweeney has very little else to add to the conclusions reached by Pearl.[1]

Professor A. M. Carr-Saunders, of the University of Liverpool, apparently attempts complete and exhaustive exploration of the population problem; he discusses its qualitative as well as its quantitative features. Since the present work is concerned only with the mode of human increase, full advantage cannot be taken of the results of his labor; comment upon much of his thoroughgoing research must be reserved for a forthcoming work on the sources and significance of quality in populations.

The whole Carr-Saunders doctrine is very neatly summed up in a few concluding sentences:

As regards quantitative problems we saw that from the first period of history onwards—from the time, that is to say, that it began to be possible for man to reap the benefits of cooperation —it was of the utmost importance for every group to approximate to the optimum number. This is the number which— taking into consideration the nature of the environment, the degree of skill employed, the habits and customs of the people concerned, and all other relevant facts—given the highest average return per head. This number is not fixed once and for all. On the contrary it is constantly varying as the conditions referred to vary, and, as skill has tended to increase throughout history, so has the number economically desirable tended to increase.[2]

[1] Sweeney, J. S., *The Population Problem*, Baltimore, 1926.

[2] Carr-Saunders, A. M., *The Population Problem,* Oxford, 1922, p. 476.

Here is the idea of an "optimum population," the *dernier cri* in population parlance, as one may find by examining Mr. Louis I. Dublin's recent population symposium [1]—though the idea is at least as old as Plato, who as every school-boy knows, suggested 5,040 as the ideal size for a city-state.

Carr-Saunders links the idea of population and production—just as we found Professor Pierson and "the optimists" doing. As a result, his ideal population is the number that would assure the greatest possible output of wealth per head, under the prevailing form of economy. This position suggests that Professor Carr-Saunders stands very near the "optimists" in their opinion that, through improvements in the technique of production, mankind has escaped—or will soon escape—the burden of the struggle for existence. Carr-Saunders, however, hastens to say: "The quantitative problem presents itself to all races at all times. There is no escaping it. The common notion that it only presents itself at certain times in certain places is based upon a failure to grasp the strength of fecundity." [2] (One finds here none of the East confusion concerning the constancy and universality of over-population.)

Carr-Saunders' formula for solving the quantitative population problem — and to a large extent the qualitative as well—is birth control:

Almost without exception those factors, which incidentally restrict increase and produce elimination, are insufficient so to reduce fertility as to keep numbers down to the optimum level. There thus arises the need for factors which directly restrict fertility and cause elimination; among primitive races these factors take the form of abortion, infanticide, and prolonged absention from intercourse. [3]

[1] Several Authors, *Population Problems*, edited by Louis I. Dublin, New York, 1926.

[2] Carr-Saunders, *loc. cit.*

[3] Carr-Saunders, *loc. cit.*

Nowhere, however, does Carr-Saunders set forth a unitary formula of population growth. He merely lays down the Platonic doctrine of an optimum population; asserts that the optimum is some function of the current rate of wealth production (suggesting strongly the hypothesis advanced in this book) and then declares that birth control is the obvious and only effective means of establishing an optimum population—or more accurately, an optimum relationship between population and production.

Mr. J. Swinburne, a British consulting engineer, has done a brilliant piece of amateur philosophizing in his *Population and the Social Problem*.[1] He sees no hope that people will ever understand what is really wrong with the world: a bad case of overpopulation. Until that is understood, nothing is of any use. No alteration in government will avail. No difference in the attitude of capital or labor can have any effect. No development in industry can do any real good. All those changes that are usually called advances only enable a larger number of people to live under a slightly readjusted scale of differing degrees of comfort and misery. Advances and discoveries in science have no more substantial meaning than a like amount of other interesting intellectual amusement. The development of a new machine, a new chemical process, or a new industry is of no permanent value to the world. Human misery is not thereby lessened. But a new hope has arisen; the solution of the problem is now developing: after four thousand years or so a change seems to be taking place in a single century.

For about seventy years the limitation of families has been practised. It began in the middle classes, and spread both up and down; and it will gradually extend until it changes the whole of the relations of society. The limitation of offspring,

---

[1] Swinburne, J., *Population and the Social Problem*, London, 1924.

and the means (to that end) form the greatest discovery man has ever made. But no one knows the discoverer, and such matters are mentioned only with bated breath.[1]

Like Carr-Saunders, Swinburne insists that all advances in material well-being are relative—meaningless, in fact, unless the increase of numbers, population, is kept in check. Stopping as he does at this point, he has however given us but a theory of poverty. For that matter, it should be recalled that even Carr-Saunders does not produce a theory of the mode of human increase. He says simply that population growth should be artificially controlled in relation to production so that the relationship shall always be at the optimum.

Instead of attempting a unitary explanation of population growth, Sir George Handley Knibbs lists seven factors which he believes govern the rate of human increase:

(1) the force of the reproductive impulse . . . . modified by contraceptive influences; (2) social traditions; (3) natural resources . . . . and the success with which they are exploited, (4) political security and economic stability; (5) distribution of sexes and ages within the population; (6) " health " of population; (7) customary age at time of marriage.[2]

If it were not for the fact that there is so wide a margin between potential fecundity (actual child-producing capacity) and the average size of families in the nations of western civilization, all of these factors could be accepted. But with potential fecundity three or four hundred per cent greater than necessary to produce families of average size, Knibbs' last three factors dwindle to insignificance. His first four points, however, sum up exactly to the formula presented and developed in these pages. With modern death rates

[1] Swinburne, J., *op. cit.*, pp. 375-77.
[2] *Shadow of the World's Future*, London, 1928, p. 36.

rapidly approaching a constant, the reproductive impulse, modified by contraceptive influences, is beyond doubt the positive controlling force in population growth. Economic forces working through psychologic channels in turn determine the extent to which the reproductive process is checked by contraceptive influences. As for the future, Knibbs sees eye to eye with East: he depicts imminent and possibly fatal consequences resulting from the future growth of population.[1]

After Carr-Saunders, Swinburne and Knibbs, it is not easy to find a post-war European who has contributed, either in fact or in opinion, to the population problem. Several books, both interesting and scholarly, have been written in Germany, in France, and in Norway, but these works add nothing to Pierson, Cassell, Nitti, Levasseur, Leroy-Beaulieu and Marshall, Professor Keynes and his colleague, Mr. H. Wright, are considered here only because Keynes is the most widely-known post-war European economist, and his colleague, because he has written a handbook on population (one of a series of publications under the general editorship of Professor Keynes) which may be considered an amplification of the few remarks Keynes has made upon the subject.

Although a European, Professor Keynes in his *Economic Consequences of the Peace* speaks in the pre-war American tone and tenor of Patten, Taussig, Seligman, Ely, and the rest—very optimistic over the present but extremely alarmed over the outlook for the very remote future. The law of diminishing returns, Keynes says, has been set aside: "Larger proportional returns from an increasing scale of production became true of agriculture as well as industry. . . . In this economic eldorado, in this economic Utopia, as the earlier economists would have deemed it, most of us

[1] Knibbs, Sir George, *Scientific American*, vol. 139, no. 4, p. 377.

were brought up." [1]   Then clouds begin to gather; Keynes sounds a high, clear note of alarm.   Population is heaping up; in fact it began to increase at an alarming rate even before the war.   Today, " Europe consists of the densest aggregation of population in the history of the world.   This population is accustomed to a relatively high standard of life, in which, even now, some sections of it anticipate improvement rather than deterioration." [2]   Here and elsewhere Keynes appears to recognize the standard of living as the one inclusive counter-agent to the effect of increasing wealth upon the growth of population—additional confirmation, in opinion at least, of the second clause of our hypothesis: populations tend to vary inversely with the level of living standards.   Further on, swinging boldly into the pessimistic strain, and referring especially to the population of Europe, he says: " Emigration is not open to the redundant surplus. For it would take years to transport them overseas, even, which is not the case, if countries could be found which were ready to receive them.   The danger confronting us, therefore, is the rapid depression of the standard of life of the European populations." [3]   That is to say, populations may not increase without a corresponding depression of living standards (assuming no increase in wealth).   Furthermore, may not the converse be inferred: a general striving for higher standards of life is the definite, all-inclusive control of population growth?

Professor Keynes' colleague, Mr. Harold Wright, does not differ materially from his more famous Cambridge associate, though he has far more to say upon the present topic in his little book on *Population*.   Mr. Wright takes a flat-out Malthusian view and then hedges his opinion, as did

[1] Keynes, J. M., *The Economic Consequences of the Peace*, New York,
[2] Keynes, J. M., *op. cit.*, p. 227.
[3] *Op. cit.*, p. 228.

Keynes and the American optimists, by saying that the Malthusian doctrine was at least temporarily set aside by nineteenth-century capitalism. Finally, however, Mr. Wright goes beyond Professor Keynes and assumes the viewpoint of leading post-war students of the population problem in advocating general birth control. Man has always been completely subject to the Malthusian principle. All his efforts could not produce enough food to provide for more than an infinitesimal part of the children that could be born. "Finding that the tortoise could not overtake the hare, primitive man seems to have done his best to persuade the hare to go to sleep, for everywhere, among primitive peoples, one at least of three devices for the limitation of numbers— abortion, infanticide, or prolonged abstention from intercourse—has been found to prevail." Further on Mr. Wright seems to stand beside East and to see Mankind at the Crossroads, for he says there are but two solutions, "two ways out, one is by increasing the productivity of labor, the other by restricting the birth-rate. Both measures appear to be necessary if the world is to be a tolerable place in the years to come."[1]

The type of theory produced by these post-war scholars is strongly propagandistic. They do not explain the mode of human increase: they merely alarm us by describing statistically or historically the actual rate of past growth; then horrify us by painting the future in the lurid colors they find upon the palette of their imaginations. Continuing however in the propagandistic, evangelistic strain, they tell us there is salvation for the repentant: birth control.

The works of these post-war theorists are not quite satisfying, yet the best of them show a sharp advance over pre-war theory, over early or late nineteenth-century doctrine; in fact, they are the most substantial works since

[1] Wright, H., *Population*, New York, 1923, p. 169.

Malthus' and Franklin's, because, like the works of Malthus and Franklin, they are rooted in biology. Any satisfying explanation of the mode of human increase must be built upon the essential theorems of biology, and developed according to the more substantial rules of economics and psychology. But at the very outset there must be a minute examination of the nature of biologic progress and of human development.

CHAPTER VI

The Life 'Struggle'—Man Appears

LIFE had persisted, down through the ages, by virtue of selfishness and by virtue of generosity. Selfishness and generosity find social expression in competition and in co-operation. If preeminence must be recognized, competition should be considered the prime force; for it seems beyond dispute that, in an overcrowded world, or conversely, in a world that contains a little less—or a great deal less—than is wanted of all good things, self concern is prerequisite to survival. There is another reason for putting individualism ahead of "cooperationism": Even in its most idealistic forms, cooperation nearly always proves to be, in final meaning, merely an indirect mode of self-regard.

Contemplation of the infinite inter-relationship of the whole life scheme is possibly the most inspiring and enthralling of human experiences—so long as one does not lift this intricate, lacework coverlet and expose the constant struggling and strangling that goes on just beneath it.

Even in their most familiar manifestions, the interrelationships of the bio-universe are amazing. Darwin tells us that cats are connected with the success of next year's clover crop. Cats determine the number of field mice. Field mice, by destroying nests and combs, regulate the number of bumble bees. Since clover blossoms are fertilized principally by bumble bees, the number of bees governs the number of fertile clover seeds. Other examples are not difficult to find, small fish, by devouring mosquito larvae, check the spread of malaria. Earthworms manufacture most of the fertile soils of the world; and white-ants or termites, working on forest borders, contribute to the alluvium of distant valleys.

The bio-universe is an infinitely intricate system of precisely balanced forces—not quite precisely balanced, for there is progress. Every part in nature is the retainer of some other part. Entirely aside then from procreative propensity or eroticism, in terms of which certain modern philosophers and psychologists needlessly try to explain all unselfishness, there is, in this essential, universal cooperation a sufficient basis for altruism.

In his tale of the leaf-cutting ants, Mr. William Beebe, an American explorer, unwinds a curious thread in the web of life. When he broke through the covering of their subterranean home, he learned the meaning of the semi-circular bits of leaf that these ants so dexterously make, and so industriously carry away to hoard. For he found immense gangs of workers chewing leaves into a green paste which becomes the culture medium for a singular fungus, heretofore unkown. This fungus is the only food of the ants while they are under ground. When the queen ant takes flight, she carried with her a small bolus of the fungus. She alights upon the earth, and soon her new brood of workers appears. When they have matured to the point where they can cut leaves and chew paste, the queen produces the fungus wad which she has planted and carefully tended for six weeks; with it she starts a new fungus culture in the leaf paste.[1]

Examples of the inter-dependence of life forms can be multiplied indefinitely; but one or two more illustrations—the first from Mr. J. Arthur Thompson—should make complete their general meaning. Everyone knows the little beetles called " death-watches " that make a tapping noise on the wainscot. The male thumps his head against the wood,

[1] Beebe, W., *Edge of the Jungle*, New York, H. Holt, 1921, p. 180.

signalling to his desired mate—speaking therefore of love not of death. The larval death-watches bore in wood and other dry materials—including books. Now, it has been shown that in the beginning of the digestive tract of the larval death-watch there are two minute pockets which are crammed with yeast plants. These work on the unpromising wood pulp; there is a tiny brewery inside the larval death-watch. Careful examination showed Professor Buchner that were no yeast-plants in the eggs of these insects; yet they were always present in the young grubs. The solution of that puzzle is almost incredible. Associated with the egg-laying apparatus in the female there are two minute reservoirs opening to the exterior, and these are full of yeast. When an egg is laid, some yeast-plants are expelled along with it, and they adhere to the rough surface of the egg shell. When the beetle-grub is ready to hatch out, it nibbles at the egg-shell, and thus its food-canal becomes infected with yeast-plants. A little leaven goes a long way with the death-watch. Details are interesting, but even more important is the general fact that a partnership of yeasts and insects had been demonstrated in scores of cases. It is no curiosity.[1]

Then there is Doctor Herandez's horned Mexican tree. This horned tree it appears is an acacia. A certain variety of ants, whose sting causes a pain that persists for a day, find homes in its horns. The " horns " are stipules, found at the base of the *pinnate* leaves. When the leaves fall, the horns remain. Ants enter the horns by boring; they cut their way through the soft pulp, eating as they go. Multiplying rapidly, they guard the acacia against browsing animals and leaf-cutting ants. Supplementing the pulp diet, there appears at the base and upon the tip of each leaf a secretion of which the ants are very fond, and which they col-

[1] *Concerning Evolution*, Yale University Press, 1925, p. 108.

lect and store in the hollowed horns.[1]   Here is a perfect partnership.   What sentimental person, noting this community interest, has an eye left for the struggle for existence—or room in his mind for belief in anything save universal cooperation?   But, as every one knows, individual organisms existed in entire independence long before (millions of generations before) there was the slightest biologic cooperation.   The selfish impulse is fundamental.   The social impulse, eons old though it is, is a new-fashioned notion compared with the primeval instinct to look out for oneself.[2]

Everywhere there is evidence that the continuity of life and of progress has been secured only through terrific over-production of every living kind.   The instinct to over-multiply—in fact to over-do everything—is essential to persistence.   Organisms, life forms that habitually under-did things were of course those that perished without reproducing their kind.   The tendency to over-do is instinctive with all organisms; but it goes deeper than that, it is a cell matter. Biologists tell us that even in the cell activity of higher organisms it is operative—that, for example, if one makes a large gash in one's flesh, the resulting scar is simply evidence, in large part, of over-healing.   If cells reproduced their kind in exactly the required proportions, an injury need leave no mark.   Though a scar may of course result from

[1] Thompson, J. A., *Concerning Evolution*, Yale Univ. Press, 1925, pp. 99-113.

[2] The current (or is it the *recent*?) school of psychologists would object of course to the use made of the word *instinct* in this and other chapters, insisting that there are a definite and closely limited number of instincts—exactly as the chemist used to insist upon a definite and closely limited number of immutable elements: sixty, seventy—or was it eighty?   But the chemist justified the atomic dogma far more convincingly than the psychologist justifies his dogma of this or that number of instincts.   One must fall back upon the merely literary use of the word.

simple mechanical distortion, it is more often entirely the resulting of over-healing. All biologic processes run to excess. Where groups of organisms are concerned the conspicuous result is excessive reproduction with constant struggle. " Nothing is easier," says Charles Darwin

than to admit in words the truth of the universal struggle for life, or more difficult—at least I have found it so—than constantly to bear this conclusion in mind. Yet, unless it be thoroughly engrained in the mind, the whole economy of nature, with every fact of distribution, rarity, abundance, extinction, and variation, will be dimly seen or quite misunderstood.[1]

The term " struggle for life " implies of course not only the efforts of individuals to survive, but the larger continuous effort of species to persist, mainly by sheer weight of numbers—prolificity—assisted however by accidental adaptation. In fact, nature seems scarcely to be interested in individuals—or even in species. All individuals perish, or at the very least, subdivide and lose their identity. Hundreds of species have been completely wiped out. Only life persists.

Of course life has never been detected apart from substance; and all life-bearing substance takes the form of discrete, discernible individuals. The individual is fundamental. Nevertheless he is invariably sacrificed and species must give way to that yet larger end: the perpetuation of life.

In visualizing the universal competition for survival, account must be taken not merely of the efforts of individuals striving to over-reach one another but also of the war between kinds, however remote their relationship, and the struggle of individuals and kinds against unfavorable inanimate circumstances. A pair of male wolves fight over a

[1] Darwin, Charles, *The Origin of Species*, London, 1885, p. 49.

kill, but the struggle may also take less apparent form: an herb clings to a dry rocky ledge, striving for water and food; bird-planted trees, may in a sense, be said to " struggle " with other trees to tempt birds to swallow their seed-bearing fruit.

Though inter-species war is perpetual the war between varieties of the *same* species is far more bitter: gray squirrels and red squirrels cannot exist long in the same woods. The mistle thrush of Scotland has caused a rapid decrease in the numbers of the song thrush. In Russia the small cock-roach has everywhere driven before it the larger variety. In Australia the imported hive bee has exterminated the small stingless bee, and the dingo has driven out the Tasmanian wolf.

But the struggle between varieties is not nearly so intense as the competition between individuals of the same kind; for these individuals must compete for the *same* things. Compare, for example, the intensity of the " struggle " between man and the giraff, man seeking the cooling shade of trees and the giraff seeking leaves of those same trees for food with the struggle for a bare living between New York or London news-vendors, between continental baggage porters —or between international dye trusts.

Competition among individuals of the human kind is by far the most bitter in all the universal struggle to go on living. The fact that nine out of ten orators, preachers and teachers rise only to urge man to restrain himself some little in undercutting and in stabbing in the back—and the existence of so many " golden rules "—are curiously overlooked bits evidencing the bitterness of human competition. In fact, does one go too far in saying that armies, hangmen, jails, governments, laws and churches constitute further evidence? In the pursuit of their ends the beasts of the field and the birds of air preserve quite a semblance of order and amity without these aids.

It is easy, of course, to paint in too lurid colors the struggle for existence—to "over-do" the nature-red-in-tooth-and-claw idea. Among plants for example, there is crowding and there is competition for sunlight, moisture, air, nitrates, phosphates and so on, but little that properly could be called struggle. It is clear, furthermore, that casual observation has over-estimated the frequency and significance of violent conflict between individual animals. Such clashes are dramatic and easily observed: they are nevertheless, curiosities. Most individuals perish from inglorious inadequacy to cope with the inanimate features of their surroundings.[1]

Darwin, noting a newly inclosed heath in Surrey where the number of self-sown firs was so great as to be unescapeably remarkable, noted in the same region uninclosed areas that were almost bare of firs. In trying to solve the mystery, he hit upon the hypothesis that seeding was prodigious everywhere, but that young trees were continually browsed down by cattle. Investigating, upon this hypothesis, he found by examining closely a square yard of heath far from the nearest clump of firs, or source of seeds, no less than thirty-two tiny trees—thirty-two seedlings within a square yard that to the glance did not contain a single fir. Here is an excellent example not only of the frantic persistence of life, but of the balanced or poised state established between species in the universal competition to persist. In this case there is an obvious competition and balance between the number of browsing animals and the number of fir trees, but it is of course a universal phenomenon, and suggests a bio-universe in which elements and forces exist in a state of almost perfect poise—not unlike the greater universe of suns, stars and planets.

[1] *Cf.* Carr-Saunders, A. M., "Biology and War," *Foreign Affairs,* April, 1929.

The way in which various elements in the bio-universe reach a balance is nicely illustrated by the goats and grey-hounds upon Juan Fernandez. The island was over-run with goats—the descendants of two or three left there by the discoverer, Juan Fernando. Spain, wishing to destroy the value of these islands as a source of food supply for the British Navy, put on shore several pairs of greyhounds. Within a short time the greyhounds had run down and killed many goats. The supply of food being temporarily plentiful, the greyhounds multiplied and only the strongest, nimblest goats, those able to flee to high rocky crags, survived. The goats however, were the principal food of the greyhounds, and their increasing scarcity made living conditions for the dogs constantly harder. Soon only the strongest and fleetest dogs were able to gain a living; many starved. The final result was of course an equilibrium between the number of greyhounds and the number of goats.

Possibly the idea of a bio-universe in which terrific forces of creation and destruction, inter-related and inter-antagonized in labyrinthic fashion, work constantly in adapting life forms to a more comfortable and extended existence deserves one further point of illumination. Paraguay offers, perhaps, precisely the instance our purpose requires. There neither cattle nor horses nor dogs have ever run wild, though to the south and north all of these species exist without the care of man. Explanation lies in the greater number (in Paraguay) of a certain fly, which lays its eggs in the navels of these animals at birth. The abundance of flies—numerous though they are—is constantly checked, probably by other parasitic insects. Therefore if certain insectivorous birds were to decrease in Paraguay, the parasitic insects would probably increase, and that would lessen the number of the navel-frequenting flies; wild cattle and horses in bordering regions would thereupon, by their natural increase, over-run Paraguay, and this would certainly greatly alter vegetation. That in turn would largely affect insects, which would affect insectivorous birds, and so onward in ever-increasing circles of complexity. But in nature, of course, the interrelationships of life are never so simple as in these isolated illustrations. War within war goes on continually, with varying success; and yet in the long run forces are so nicely balanced that the face of nature remains for long periods of time apparently uniform—though the merest trifle might give overwhelming victory to one species or to another.

The bio-universe is not perfectly poised: there is progress. Progress furthermore is not accident; it is indispensable, a condition to existence. Concurrent building up and breaking down, the central characteristic of life forms, decrees progress—or extinction. This process, or principle, acts in all that is organic or of an organic nature: in cells, in tissue, in organs, in individuals, in institutions, in society as a whole: concurrent building up and breaking down, everywhere, universal to life. But always one outruns the other. There is no absolutely poised state in life: there is decay or growth. Progress is essential to life. The persistence of life is in itself adequate evidence of adaptation, of progress.

A complete grasp of at least the outlines of the bio-universe, with its intricate relationships of bitter competition and expedient cooperation, is indispensable to an understanding of the mode of animal increase. Overlying an obvious similarity in the modes of animal increase and human increase, there is an extremely significant difference. Between the intelligence of man and the intelligence of the next mostly highly cerebrated animal lies the widest gap in the entire scale of biologic development. Man is the thinking animal. This differentiating character and its product in culture and civilization should be studied, so far as possible, from that remote day when man first emerged in the general welter of life.

Is life simply a pattern, an arrangement, or it is an independent reality? No one knows. It may be that life is a thing apart from matter and motion; many professing biologists of the first order incline strongly to that opinion. Many others, perhaps a majority, incline however to the opposed view; that life or animate substance is simply an aspect or state of the inanimate—merely, some curious happening, in the remotest past, set lifeless substance to rebuilding at a rate slightly exceeding the rate at which it was breaking down, an accident, a trick, a curious inter-play of molecules, atoms, and attractive and repellent forces.

According to evolutionary doctrine, man or his primordial ancestor was present in the original batch of lifeless substance that first took on the life trick, the trick of simultaneously building up and breaking down, of building outside substance into its own substance.[1] This promordial ancestor was at first a simplest Protist, a microscopic drop of jelly, possessing however a miraculously intricate nucleus, which, according to recent theory must have contained, in quintessential form, the entire future of the race. Life appeared on this planet probably 200,000,000 years ago—possibly 1,000,000,000 years ago.

Down through the ages, down through the years in their hundreds, in their thousands, in their millions, went this tiny precursor of humanity, dividing, re-dividing, increasing, multiplying with unbelievable extravagance, meeting everywhere ruthless, unsparing destruction: changing, developing, progressing—though by no more than a millionth's of a hairsbreadth, so to speak, from age to age—and finally prevailing.

[1] Osborn, Henry Fairfield, *The Origin and Evolution of Life*, New York, 1917.

It is by no means certain, however, that the man ancestor assumed at any time the form of this or that postulated " step " in the biologic ladder; in fact it is reasonably certain that there were no " steps "—the evolutionary hypothesis of biologic progress, even as modified by the theory of mutants, describes a continuous process. The human ancestor passed through an infinite, or inexpressibly great number of life forms which may or may not have approximated in contour, structure and functioning certain existing life forms. Quite obviously however, one may not say that man descended from this or that organism—though the man strain may have assumed, at some stage in its development, a similar form.

The primate ancestor of mankind—and of other primate species—" appeared ", or passed through the generalized primate form, in what geologists call Eocene times, that is to say about twenty million years ago. " Man appears "— or rather the man stock, or strain passed into the man form possibly fifteen million years later, though no slightest objective evidence or relic of man's existence earlier than one or two million years ago has thus far been discovered.

Although the remains of several individual members of pre-historic populations have been uncovered, these relics are of slight significance in a study of population growth. Far more concerning the increase of pre-historic populations may be inferred from the lives of modern primitives than from the direct evidence of the few human bones and teeth that have been preserved and brought down through the ages. But much may be learned from the cultural remains of ancient populations.

In studying the cultural remains of pre-historic populations it is easy to gain the mistaken impression that a considerable degree of organization and skill in art and manufacture was attained by very ancient peoples. Their art, especially in its inceptions, was largely accidental. Many striking artifacts grew out of materials taken from nature in almost their final state: a touch or a stroke or two, here and there brought out final utility or complete esthetic value.

It is customary to divide early cultures into four principal periods: the Old Stone, the New Stone, the Bronze and the Iron Ages. The Old Stone culture, which lasted four or five hundred thousand years, ended about twenty thousand years ago. It is distinguished from the New Stone culture by the fact that its implements were not polished; agriculture was not practiced; pottery was not made; animals were not domesticated. All of these things were accomplished by the New Stone Age populations. But preceding all of these culture periods many students would include an Eolithic stage.[1]

The Eolithic period is marked by eoliths, rough implements—so rough in fact that some shadow of doubt is thrown over their origin. They may or may not have been produced by human hands. Or if it is assumed that they were produced by natural agencies, they may or may not have been selected from nature for human purposes. In brief, they may be accidents of nature entirely dissociated from human use or purpose. The first geuine artifacts or implements of undoubted human origin were found in surroundings which indicate that they were used about 150,000 years ago.[2]

At that time, man began making his home in caves. He used fire. (There are however traces of a much earlier use of fire). Ceremonial burial was practiced. The La Chapelle-Aux-Saints skeleton, for example, indicated by its position that the body had been carefully placed in burial.

[1] Osborn, *Men of the Old Stone Age*, New York, 1915, p. 270 *et seq.*
[2] MacCurdy, G., *Human Origins*, New York, 1924, pp. 86-110.

Articles of use were found near the skeleton. One nicely moulded implement lay within reach of the left hand.[1]

Old Stone culture reached its greatest pitch in the middle of the late Palaeolithic period—slightly more than 20,000 years ago. It is this period which produced the slim and sharply pointed willow-leaf and laurel-leaf lance heads. Bone tools appeared for the first time. Ceremonies of various sorts became established, and if there was no belief in a future life in the modern meaning of that phrase, there were certainly traditional beliefs regarding the state of the deceased. The most remarkable cultural remains of the late Palaeolithic period are the drawings and paintings found upon the walls of caves. They were made throughout a long range of years and indicate a high degree of skill and taste—though it is possible that under the magic touch of recent popular authors their significance has been overemphasized.[2]

This peak of cultural development was succeeded in the twilight of the Old Stone Age by a culture that was obviously degenerate. Bone and stone implements began to show poor workmanship; artistic creations vanished, and although some new tricks of civilization made their appearance—for example the domestication of the dog—there was a marked regression in man's mode of living.

The dawn of the New Stone culture brought the first clumsy groping of early agriculture and the profitable domestication of animals; a number of cereals were cultivated; the grape was nurtured and possibly fruit trees as well; the polishing of stone implements began; linen and pottery were manufactured. It is generally agreed that these advances represent a cultural invasion from the East. In fact,

[1] Osborn, *Men of the Old Stone Age*, New York, 1915, p. 216.

[2] Keath, Sir Arthur, *The Antiquity of Man*, Philadelphia, 1915, pp. 61-109; MacCurdy, G., *Human Origins*, New York, 1924, pp. 172 *et seq.*

throughout the story of mankind, from the remotest trace of earliest civilization to a date well within historic times, the course of culture was westward. It is not possible to date the earliest backwash of culture from West to East: it is rather clear however, that Asia learned nothing from Europe until some time after the invention of gunpowder—scarcely more than four hundred years ago.[1]

From the point of view of the present study, the striking feature of the New Stone, or Neolithic Age was its great progress in economic and in general social development. Neolithic man became comparatively rich and lived in villages of some size—social man and economic man appeared.

Some slight social organization can be inferred as early as Old Stone or Palaeolithic times, for the degree of skill expressed in Palaeolithic weapons and implements could not have been acquired without organization and social intercourse. The achievements of late Paleolithic man also indicate a substantial amount of tradition, and tradition is of course a social product. Probably the general tendency is toward considering the life of early man far more primitive than it actually was. In all probability life was in fact no more primitive than with many backward tribes extant early in the twentieth century. Though it is of course ridiculous to attempt to date accurately the "appearance" of society or civilization, it is fair to say that the rudiments of social organization were developing during a period extending from 150,000 to 50,000 years ago.

Of paramount significance in a population study, trade routes were opened in Neolithic times. Some of these routes brought Baltic populations into communication with the Mediterranean. The famous Brenner pass became the summit of a highway beginning in Venice and reaching the Danube by way of the Inn; it penetrated Bohemia's forests

[1] Keith, A., *The Antiquity of Man*, Philadelphia, 1915, p. 2 *et seq.*

and by way of the Moldau reached the Elbe which it followed to the sea.

It is far from clear just when and where the first use was made of metal—probably gold, for it is found in many regions in the pure or metallic state, and its lustre attracts attention. All than can be said with certainty is that the use of metals originated in the East, probably about 5000 B. C.—possibly some two or even three thousand years earlier.[1] The important point for present consideration is that the use of metals and the development of civilization were synchronized. With the use of metals came highly organized mass fights (wars), clothes, commerce, large huddled masses of humanity (cities), and the ostentatious use of wealth—as distinguished from its use merely as a means of mitigating the rigors of existence. These are the most conspicuous features of what we have come to call civilization.

The back-bone of civilization is made of iron. It is a mistake however, to assume that there was no civilization before iron. The pomp and power of the Minoan civilization, the glorious period of Egyptian history, the great Sumerian civilization and the beginnings of Babylonian and Assyrian splendor all came before iron, it is not even clear that the present civilization bases its origin and early development upon the use of iron. Other innovations, the earliest use of the wheel and of the plow, for example, were more significant; the invention of writing was certainly of equal importance. It is quite conceivable that modern civilization could have developed in large part—though perhaps in slightly different shape—without the use of iron. At this date however, civilization would of course crumble were its iron hastily withdrawn.

About 1400 B. C., in southwestern Asia, iron was prob-

---

[1] Osborn, *Men of the Old Stone Age*, New York, 1915, p. 18.

ably used for the first time—certainly in any practical sense. The earliest known Egyptian iron weapon is usually dated 1200 B. C.   Three hundred years later iron entered Europe; it reached Scandinavia and England in about 500 B. C. Iron took a thousand years in crossing Europe.   So slow— even during this comparatively recent period—was the western march of culture.

At this point the cumulative nature of the development of civilization should be underlined.   The Old Stone culture extended over more than 100,000 years; the magnificently improved New Stone Age took but 10,000 years for its development; the subtle bronze culture was brought to its apogee in less than 2,000 years.   The cumulative nature of modern progress is too apparent to need emphasis.

One further fact of extreme significance must be pointed out: in historic times man has not made the slightest discernible biologic progress.   All recent human progress lies in the cumulative multiplication of mental tricks and of machinery.[1]   It is a pity that more complete evidence of the nature of early economic and social life has not been uncovered, for it would be of considerable value in the present study.

An examination of the circumstances of man's emergence in the bio-universe and a review of the development of prehistoric human life has revealed nothing to indicate that the mode of increase of early populations, surveyed in the large —that is to say, sociologically—differed in any significant way from the mode of animal increase.   In later chapters a particular, or biological, study of human increase and animal increase will be made, but this larger, sociological view must be continued to determine, if possible, whether modern populations have escaped the effect and burden of the laws of animal increase.

[1] Conklin, E. G., *The Direction of Human Evolution*, New York, 1921, pp. 71-72.

CHAPTER VII

The Struggle Continues

An observer peers through the quiet waters of a shallow estuary and sees a colony of hermit crabs distributed over its floor; he sees also an exact analogy of the human economic struggle. A bit of food drifts to the bottom. With magic swiftness one of these small beasts, quicker than the rest, leaves his stolen home, or tiny curling shell, and scoops the morsel. During the instant " his " home is vacant, another crab deserts a cracked or badly-fitting shell and appropriates the shelter of the food gatherer. Not satisfied with the profit of his first theft, he nestles comfortably in his new shell, maneuvring it the while to a point that offers the possibility of despoiling the first crab of a portion of his meal.

It is only with effort that human beings can convince themselves—and remain convinced—that they are animals, and that little can be said of cat or dog or wolf or even snake that cannot be said of any of us—or of our friends or enemies. Unthinking persons—especially optimists—feel that the man kind, unlike other life forms, has escaped the rigor and ruthlessness of the struggle to persist. Thinking persons and others who have no high opinion of themselves take an opposite view. Even a cursory examination of the facts of population growth, human wants, and the available supply of goods and services is instantly convincing.

The minimum-of-subsistence [1] level in the United States

[1] Minimum of subsistence here means the minimum of income that will insure economically efficient living.

(1927) for the families of factory workers is about $1450 in the South and $1650 in the North.[1] Factory workers in Southern cotton mills receive on the average not more than $1100 a year.[2] In New England mill towns, corresponding figures suggest quite as bitter a struggle.

A New York investigator found in 1917 (a year when employment conditions were better than average), that a rise in the price of milk from nine to fourteen cents a quart compelled seventy per cent of the poorer families to reduce their purchase of milk. Even before the increase in price, these families were taking only half the amount of milk essential to health.[3]

In 1927 Doctor Leila Houghteling made a study of income and the standard of living in a group made up of families of 467 unskilled laborers in Chicago. The heads of these families were of the better grade of laborers; all had been carried continuously on the books of their employers for at least one year and many were doing highly specialized work.[4] Doctor Houghteling found that seventy per cent were earning less than the amount necessary to support their families on the minimum of subsistence level. In nearly half of the 467 families, the earnings of mother, father and children combined fell short of the minimum of subsistence.[5]

Even in the richest nations, and in periods of general prosperity there are families whose incomes are below the subsistence line. These families do not lack this or that comfort or luxury; they lack proper food. Rent must be paid;

[1] Bossard, J. H. S., *Problems of Social Well-Being*, New York, 1927, pp. 50-55.

[2] Blanshard, P., *The Nation*, vol. cxxviii, p. 580.

[3] Roberts, L. J., *Nutrition Work with Children*, Chicago, 1927, p. 132.

[4] Houghteling, L., *Income and Standard of Living*, Chicago, 1923, pp. 17-20.

[5] *Op. cit.*, pp. 80 and 83.

a certain minimum of clothes must be provided for father and children, so that they may go to work and to school; the only cut than can be made is in food. The result is chronic undernourishment.[1]

A long list of American investigators have found that, on the average, children in prosperous localities are taller and heavier than children living in poorer regions. This can mean only that, in the most favored nations of the world, the struggle for existence not only continues but it leaves a large section of the population in what may be called —in happier age—a semi-starved condition.[2]

The greater prevalence of sickness among the poor is further evidence of a scarcity of material good things and of the reality of struggle. A health study conducted among 4,161 wage earners in the United States in May and June of 1916 showed sickness to be five times as frequent among the most poorly paid workers as among those a little less than twice as well paid.[3] Tuberculosis is far more prevalent among the poor than among the rich. Certain diseases are almost unknown except among the very poor.

It has been extimated that one-fourth of the school children in the United States are badly nourished. Early studies of the physical well-being of school children attributed malnutrition almost entirely to poverty, but that was a mistake. Roberts says, ' The extent to which poverty causes malnutrition has not been determined, but it is undoubtedly true that many children would be better nourished if their parents had an income that would enable the family to have sufficient air and sunlight and an adequate diet.[4]

[1] Roberts, L. J., Nutrition Work with Children, Chicago, 1927, p. 132.

[2] Baldwin, B. T., The Physical Growth of Children, Iowa City, 1921 and Roberts, op. cit.

[3] U. S. Public Health Reports, vol. xxxiii, no. 47, November, 1918.

[4] U. S. Department of Labor, Children's Bureau, Bulletin Publ'n No. 59, 1927, pp. 5, 9.

In 1919, the minimum of subsistence for working-men's families in the United States appears to have been about $1550.[1] In that same year $1300 was found to be the average wage received by 405,000 workers surveyed by the United States Bureau of Labor Statistics.[2] Such a discrepancy between the value of the commodities and services necessary to life and the means of securing those necessities, (in a nation where welfare runs at a comparatively high level) suggests that at the passing moment the vast majority of human beings the world over have not the means of maintaining themselves in an efficient state; and that, with the intricacies of modern economic relations making every one's business a concern of every other person, it is fair to say that the entire human kind is in the universal life struggle.

Never has world population increased so rapidly as during the early years of the twentieth century.[3] We have just learned that the man kind " appeared " more than 500,000 years ago. In all that time, breeding with no regard for anything but momentary appetite, the ruthlessness and rigors of nature left, in the year 1800 A. D., but 850,000,000 people. In the succeeding century—a few clock-ticks compared with the ages that went before—population doubled, exceeded 1,750,000,000. During the first quarter of the twentieth century, population increased at a rate of about one per cent a year—15,000,000 additional mouths to feed every time the earth swung round the sun. Figuring on the basis of a thousand pounds of dry food-stuffs per adult per year and allowing for ordinary loss and for seed, the farmers of the world must produce each year additional

---

[1] Bossard, J. H. S., *Problems of Social Well-Being*, New York, 1927.

[2] Douglas, Hitchcock and Atkins, Chicago, 1923, *The Worker in Modern Economic Societies*, p. 302.

[3] Ross, E. A., *Standing Room Only?* New York, 1927, p. 102.

food-stuffs to the extent of 23,000,000,000 pounds—merely to maintain the world in its present state of hunger.[1]

From what obscure source will the land come upon which this additional food must grow? Under average agricultural conditions three acres are required to support one man. Every year therefore, 40,000000 tillable acres must be added to the farm area of the earth—a difficult job—and, since good land is taken up first, every new acre has of course a little less productive power than the one that came before it.[2]

As late as the nineteenth century, famines were frequent in Asia. In fact, writing in 1919, Mr. J. Russell Smith says, " Within this century human bones have been taken to the Indian fertilizer factories by the trainload, because whole populations had perished, and not even the most distant kin of the dead remained on earth to bury them." [3] In ancient days recurrent famine was universal. This all-devouring monster, with its tenuous tongue, licked up its thousands quite as the relentless ant-eater decimates an ant colony. Then came improvements in transportation, agriculture and the storage of supplies; in consequence famines have been abated. Today, except in the Far East—where they are becoming less frequent—famines are unknown.

Transportation however did not obliterate hunger, but merely spread it out a little more thinly. Modern commerce did not free mankind from the struggle to go on living. Population pressure became slightly less acute in certain spots, and the struggle in those regions became more polite. Products of manufacture were exchanged for food brought from newly opened, distant lands; Nature's scanty dining table was enlarged; but the flood gates of over-propagation

[1] East, E. M., *Mankind at the Cross Roads*, New York, 1923, p. 67.
[2] *Idem*, p. 68.
[3] *The World's Food Resources*, H. Holt Co., New York, 1919.

remained open; a steady trickle of new population became
a torrent which filled all seats at table, leaving many a poor
Lazarus struggling for crumbs.   Bosard reports, for example, that the gathering of fuel in the streets, on railway
embankments and similar places is far more general than
is supposed.   More than half of the families living on or
below the minimum of subsistence level (which includes
about half of the families of unskilled laborers) obtain part
of their fuel in this way.[1]

According to Knibbs, the population of the world doubles
every sixty years.   Maintaining that rate through the next
three generations would bring into the struggle for existence 7,000,000,000 in a world which today is crowded with
1,900,000,000—and in the year 3000 A. D. the population
of the world would be 34,000,000,000.   It has been calculated that if—even at the present time—the entire food production of the world were distributed equally, everyone
would lack one-third the amount of proteids necessary to
produce the energy required for efficient living:[2] rather
clear evidence that the man kind has not escaped the universal struggle to remain alive.

Kelso finds that, " Population presses always against the
upward limit of subsistence; for which reason any unex-
pected limitation of food forces some stomachs to remain
empty.   It is this condition of the human struggle that is
the mother of wars and the basic cause of poverty.   While
it shall obtain, poverty in greater or less degree is assured." [3]

Not only is it clear that man has not escaped the rigors of
the struggle for existence, but there is a great deal of evi-

[1] Bossard, J. H. S., *Problems of Social Well-Being*, New York, 1927,
p. 92.

[2] Bland, J. O. P., " Population and Food Supply," *Edinburgh Review*,
vol. 227, p. 247 (footnote).

[3] Kelso, R. W., *Poverty*, New York, 1929, p. 33.

dence to show that the struggling has become ever more rigorous for all except the fortune-favored minority.   In the
United States it is estimated that on the average fifteen to
twenty-five per cent of the population exist below the level
of well-being at which one can replenish fully the forces of
life as they are consumed in toil.   Twenty per cent of the
people of the United States are living in part, upon their
physical, or health, capital.[1]

In the winter of 1917-18, the Department of Health of
New York City studied the effect of rising prices upon the
well-being of 2,000 workmen's families.   In nine per cent
of these families women went to work for the first time; the
same proportion of families sought charity for the first time;
eighteen per cent went into debt; six per cent took in board-
ers for the first time; thirty-seven per cent eliminated meat
from their diet, and an additional seventeen per cent reduced
the amount of meat purchased; forty per cent eliminated
eggs; thirty per cent gave up butter; six per cent gave up
sugar; and fifteen per cent stopped taking milk.   All of this,
be it remembered, was not the result of unemployment, not
even the result of part-time or lowered wages: employment
conditions were, at the time, excellent: It was the result
merely of an increase in prices.[2]

Gillin finds that even before the War, two and one-half
per cent of the population of the United Kingdom were
paupers, officially considered.   The actual extent of poverty
was of course much greater, probably five to eight per cent.
During the decade following the War, when there were a
million and a half men continually out of employment, the
extent of actual poverty must at times have amounted to
nearly one out of every five persons in the population.   Ac-

[1] Bossard, J. H. S., *Problems of Social Well-Being*, New York, 1927,
p. 94.

[2] Harris, L. I., *American Journal of Public Health*, July, 1919.

cording to Gillin's figures, it is fair to assume that ten per cent of the people of the United States exist in a state of dangerous exposure to the forces that destroy life.[1] Parmelle, who defines the state of poverty as any exposure to the forces of destruction that can be attributed to insufficient income, finds that nearly fifty per cent of all families in the United States exist in a state of poverty.[2] Kelso's testimony follows: " We may conclude that the unskilled laborers of America live in poverty; and that of those who work with their hands and are nevertheless skilled, from a third to a half possess neither the means nor the potentiality for the maintenance of a minimum standard of social competency." [3]

Furthermore, experts testify that *without conscious control of population growth* there is every promise that the struggle for existence will become far more bitter than anything so far experienced. The greatest rate of food-producing efficiency attainable (a rate that would utilize two and a half acres per person) would require forty per cent of the earth's surface to maintain a population of 5,200,-000,000—a population which, at the present rate of increase, would be reached, according to Professor East, in a little more than a century.[4] At that time, says East, " the world would be filled with people without faith or hope, a seething mass of discontented humanity struggling for mere existence." [5]

Today, few nations of Western civilization are " self-sup-

[1] Gillin, J. L., *Poverty and Dependency* (Rev'd Ed'n), New York, 1926, pp. 37-41.

[2] Parmelle, M., *Poverty and Social Progress*, New York, 1916, p. 63.

[3] Kelso, R. W., *op. cit.*, p. 54.

[4] East, E. M., *Mankind at the Cross Roads*, New York, 1923, pp. 69 and 70.

[5] *Op. cit.*, p. 70.

porting ". By *self-supporting* nations economists usually mean those which produce enough of the fundamental necessities of life to keep their populations at a high level of physical efficiency. Though England, for example, produces a large quantity of wealth in manufactured goods, transportation services and financial services, which may be exchanged for food and other fundamentals, she is not considered self-supporting. Even the United States, for many generations one of the principal food sources of the Western World, went over, during the second quarter of the twentieth century, to the column of non-self-supporting states. During the year 1927, the United States of North America imported a larger food value in calories than they exported.[1] As early as 1912 the United States, from being the largest purveyor of meat to the United Kingdom, reached the point of having none to export and became an importer of Australian mutton and South American beef.[2] With the exception of Russia, leading European nations long ago became partly dependent upon outside sources for the fundamental requisites of life.[3] East estimates for example, that Germany is seventy-two per cent self-supporting; France, seventy per cent; Italy, sixty-four per cent, and Belgium, thirty-seven per cent. If these figures, based quite likely upon data now nearly twenty years old, were to be modernized, they should all have to be revised sharply downward.

It is of course indisputable, as McFall points out, that the mere fact that nations of our Western Civilization are no longer " self-supporting " does not mean that they could not raise sufficient food for their populations if they wished.[4]

[1] *Commerce Monthly*, May, 1928 (Pub. of the National Bank of Commerce, New York).

[2] Bland, J. O. P., *Edinburgh Review*, vol. 227 : 246.

[3] Leroy-Beaulien, *La Question de la Population*, Paris, 1913, pp. 83-86.

[4] McFall, R. J., *Yale Review*, vol. 15 (n. s.), pp. 298-299.

Quite true; but if these nations were to concentrate upon producing food instead of the more highly valued articles of commerce which they at present produce and exchange for food, standards of living everywhere would have to be reduced. Standards of living, especially those items in the standards of living that satisfy mainly the ego, are however the last things that modern populations are willing to sacrifice. Modern man and modern woman will give up woolens, meat, butter, eggs; they will send their children to school improperly clothed; but they will not sacrifice the things they consider necessary to the full life of their social class.

Patterson recalls furthermore the post-war outburst of nationalism, with its jacking up of tariff barriers and consequent paralysis of international commerce. The benefit of the principle pointed out by McFall of course fails in the same proportion that world trade is impeded. Patterson continues, " There are already so many people in Western Europe that living-standards there must be materially and permanently depressed unless business relations can be effectively maintained within Europe and between Europe and other parts of the world." [1]

Many persons believe that the rigors of the struggle for existence might be somewhat softened and were we to look seaward for new sources of food. They however overlook the fact that in the seas as well as on land, plants are the primary foods. Every mouthful of animal derivatives that one eats is grass—whether it is the eel-grass of the sea or one of the more familiar land grasses. A cow, for example, may be considered a machine for turning grass into beef, milk, butter, cheese and other food products. In the same way, a sturgeon is a machine for converting eel-grass into

---

[1] Patterson, E. M., *Europe in 1927, An Economic Survey*, Philadelphia, 1927, p. 4.

fish cutlets or caviar. Sometimes grass passes through two or three machines before it becomes human food; that is, where a food animal or fish feeds upon the cousins of its kind. All of this leads us to the obvious conclusion that sea-life is limited absolutely by the supply of grass, which is almost entirely confined to a strip of water near shore, extending not far beyond the thirty-fathom life—for light is of course essential to the existence of most plant life, and below thirty fathoms the sea is in darkness. Although sea areas are in total vastly greater than land areas, it has been estimated that the nutriment-producing capacity of the sea—even if it could be wholly utilized—does not amount to more than five per cent of the nutriment-producing capacity of land areas. It has also been estimated that not more than one-tenth of one per cent of the food value contained in sea plants could actually be converted into suitable form, and captured for human use.[1]

Little then can be looked for from the sea to ameliorate the struggle to live. On land the ultimate limit of soil fertility is being rapidly reached. The inevitable law of diminishing returns is working in every direction, which is to say we are finding everywhere that, whereas it may cost but twice as much to make two blades of grass grow where one grew before, it costs slightly more than say *five* times as much to coax two other blades of grass to grow in that same area. East agrees with Ross' view that the population of the world is rising at the most rapid rate in history. This view however has not been proven. It is not quite certain that the high standards of living demanded almost universally in this second quarter of the twentieth century are not already slowing down the rate of human increase. There is nevertheless very little in the relation of population

[1] *Cf.* Martin, G. W., "The Food Resources of the Sea," *Scientific Monthly*, vol. 15: 455-467.

growth to probable future food supply to indicate that man has escaped the struggle for existence or that, assuming no change in his attitude toward the population problem, his struggle for existence will change in any way except to become more severe.

Many persons point to the arctic and antarctic as possible sources of additional food. Let us quote Stefansson, the greatest of all enthusiasts in the development of polar regions, speaking particularly of the possible future production of reindeer meat: " As an absolute quantity this means a large supply of meat, but relatively to the demands of the world as the world is today it is not large. With reference to the world of a hundred years from now on, if we avoid destructive wars and do not adopt birth-control, this supply, vast in itself, will be insignificant."

The food supply of the world can be increased. Of that there is no doubt. Each increment however will be gained at constantly greater cost. The law of diminishing returns has not been annulled. " From now on," says Leschoier, " extension of crop acreage must come through irrigation of semi-deserts, drainage of swamps, reclamation of cut-over lands, conquest of tropic forests, swamps, and jungles, and the ploughing-up of pasture." [1]

It is futile to quote more widely from authority, to multiply by two or three or ten, instances already cited as type cases of the views of experts concerning the future state of the world's larder. The principal currents of authoritative opinion impel strongly the conclusion that the struggle for existence, far from having disappeared, as, in meaning if not in surface appearance, just what it has always been— and there is room for the opinion that the struggle for existence is more intense than ever. As Jean-Baptiste Say

[1] *Population Problems in the United States and Canada* (Dublin editor), New York, 1926, p. 79.

has phrased it: *Partout ou l'on produit un pain nait un homme.*

From the study of life in its broadest aspects, detailed in a preceding chapter and from the sociological study just concluded, the main outlines of the modes of animal increase and of human increase, their points of similarity and their points of difference, have begun to appear.   Nevertheless it is obvious that to determine the nature of the underlying biologic forces which govern population growth, a more particular, an almost purely biologic study of the nature of animal and of human increase, must be undertaken.

CHAPTER VIII

ANIMAL INCREASE

GROWTH and reproduction are one. The growth of population does not differ significantly from the growth of individual animals or plants.[1]

With the unicellulars, the tiniest of life forms, growth is, so far as the biologist can tell us, a mere matter of spontaneous swelling. This may or may not be true, but it is quite certain that with the higher or more complicated life forms, growth is a matter of multiplication. The cells of a full-grown tree or of a man are substantially the same as the cells of the corresponding seed or embryo. Merely there are more, enormously more, cells. All but the tiniest of life forms increase in bulk through the multiplication of cells. Therefore to discover the mode of animal increase we must first examine the nature of growth.

Since all growth of which the biologist has any very clear understanding is, as we have said, a matter of cell division— or multiplication—let us look into that basic matter. Why does a cell, a tiny bit of jelly-like substance with an incredibly complex and significant center of nucleus, divide— and thereby, multiply? It does so to increase its surface. The surface of a cell not only defines its form, but its life as well. Through it, the cell comes into relation with its surroundings, obtains nourishment, receives stimulation, gives out waste materials and secretions. If a cell were to

[1] Pearl, R., *The Biology of Population Growth*, New York, 1928, p. 10.

grow indefinitely, its surface would soon become inadequate. (Those of us who remember our solid geometry recall that surface increases as the square, the second power, of the diameter; while volume, or content, increases as the cube, third power, of the diameter.)   Beyond a certain point, therefore, growth would bring starvation or inadequate excretion.   To avoid this, the cell divides and thereby gains in surface without at the same time enlarging its volume.   The volume of two daughter cells, at the instant of division, is of course equal to that of the parent, but their total surface is far greater than the surface of the parent cell.

A simple, all-inclusive, if somewhat roughly generalizing method of measuring growth is by recording weight at regular intervals of time.   Careful and complete studies have been made of the growth of guinea pigs and albino rats, and less complete studies of human growth.   Shown graphically, data indicating rate of growth follows in every case the path of a stretched-out S-shaped curve.   That is to say, gains are at first small, but increasing continually; then they begin to diminish and finally disappear.   This stretched-out S-shaped curve of growth is precisely the curve which East and Pearl agree depicts the growth of populations—ancient populations, modern populations, advanced populations, backward populations, fruit-fly populations and colonies of yeast plants.[1]

Diagrams showing weights recorded at regular intervals of time are, however, thoroughly unsatisfactory, for they do not indicate *rate* of growth nor permit direct comparison. Obviously, for a new-born babe to gain an ounce is a far greater achievement than for a husky lad who weighs ten times as much.

[1] *Cf.* East, E. M., *Mankind at the Crossroads*, New York, 1923, pp. 150-2; Pearl, Raymond, *The Biology of Population Growth*, New York, 1925, pp. 5-21.

To measure *rate* of growth Minot constructed a diagram showing the *percentage* of gain in weight made during equal, successive intervals: the gain in weight during the first month, for example, is shown as a percentage of weight at the end of the first month, and so on. Presented thus, the curve of growth takes on a form very unlike the S-shaped diagram. It now appears that from birth, rate of growth constantly diminishes. From a high initial rate of growth there is a continuous decline. The curve depicting this decline is steep at first, then gradually flattens out until growth ceases entirely.[1]

Mode of growth is essentially the same for a human being, a rat, a guinea pig, a rabbit, or a radish. Furthermore, the same character appears in the mode of population growth, and for that matter the mode of variation of all data yielding the S-shaped curve; for it will be instantly recognized that this is a matter of mathematics — not of biology — and that the application of the same mathematical process to similar data will always yield similar results. The rate of growth, then, for all population groups, under approximately constant economic conditions, is precisely the constantly decreasing one which holds for the growth of organisms and which, we remember, finally slows down and stops.

The same rule applies to intra-uterine life. The human ovum at the instant of fertilization is a tiny sphere two-tenths of a millimeter in diameter. Just before birth the human embryo is a billion times its size at conception.[2] During the first year of independent life there is a gain of only two hundred per cent in weight, during the second year there is a gain of twenty per cent, during the third year

[1] *Op. cit.*, pp. 101-130.
[2] Woodruff, A. A., *Foundation of Biology*, New York, 1922, p. 16.

growth amounts to no more than twelve per cent. With
the exception of a slight disturbance at the age of puberty,
the rate diminishes steadily, amounting finally to about two
per cent in the nineteenth year.[1]

It is strikingly apparent then that the growth of organisms
and the growth of populations are similar: one is a matter
of the multiplication of cells and the other the multiplication
of individuals. From a study of these similar processes one
is strongly impelled toward the conclusion that, from the
beginning—excepting disturbances due to radical changes in
economy — a high initial rate of population growth has
slowed down continually and will finally cease altogether.

A further point of similarity in the growth of individual
organisms and of populations appears. At the time the
chick breaks the egg (or for mammals, at the time of birth)
there is a rude dislocation, or break in the continuity of the
curve of growth. This is precisely the effect recorded in
Pearl's curve of population increase at points where populations take on a radically different mode of economy—for
example, the point at which a nation enters "the machine
age."

From whatever source the primary impetus may come,
rate of growth in an individual is bound to be mathematically related to the rate of food assimilation and the process
of oxidation—just as population growth is mathematically
related to birth rates and death rates.

As with propagating power, growth is partly a matter of
heredity, but even growth may be controlled, to an extent,
in many ways. Fluctuations in the size of populations may
of course be governed by far simpler means.

Gudernatsch, feeding the secretion of the thymus gland
to tadpoles, found growth greatly accelerated. The pineal

[1] Minot, *op. cit.*, pp. 101-130.

gland, situated almost exactly in the geometrical center of the brain, affects development and growth. It appears to govern the retention or loss of infantile characters. When removed or degenerated, stature increases rapidly and the genitals develop precociously. There are cases of boys of five or six years having the sexual development of boys of eighteen, and the mentalities of men. Unfortunately, mental precocity referable to this cause—pineal insufficiency—is of short duration, for death is usually early. Feeding the extract of this organ induces growth, development and strength. That the reproductive glands of the male affect growth, is shown by the greater than normal stature of eunuchs.

Diet affects growth. Nowhere is the effect of diet upon growth and development more strikingly exhibited than in the production of queen bees. Queens differ from workers in many respects, especially in size and ability to produce eggs. All bees, however, develop from precisely similar larvæ. At the age of two or three days, a few larvæ are removed from worker cells to more commodious, queen cells. They are fed a highly nitrogenous food—partly pre-digested by workers—called royal jelly. This diet seems to produce ovaries. Other changes in structure and size take place and the queens become markedly different from workers.

It is not possible to say exactly which foods promote and which retard human growth. It is known, however, that lard, olive oil and certain other vegetable fats, for example, lack some growth-producing substance or quality possessed by butter. Other more apparent substances, proteins and certain inorganic salts, have been proven definitely to assist growth. When they are lacking, growth is retarded. By regulating precisely vitamin content, fat content and the amount of pure proteins in diet, physiologists have been able to control very accurately the rate of growth of animals. Osborne and Mendel have kept albino rats at a practically constant weight from thirty to more than five hundred days. One female rat that weighed fifty-three grams at the age of thirty-nine days gained but six grams during the next four hundred and seventy-four days. Normally the gain should have been about one hundred and fifty grams. This represents suspension of growth for a period comparable in the human species to nearly twice the period during which growth normally occurs.[1]

Furthermore, Osborn and Mendel showed that when growth was suspended far past the end of the normal growing period, adequate diet brings renewed growth and, ultimately, normal size. Indeed, one male rat whose weight was allowed to increase only twenty-one grams between the ages of thirty-five and three hundred and three days, actually attained a weight of three hundred and seventy-six grams, although the average for males was but three hundred grams. This rat ultimately reached a weight corresponding to one hundred and eighty-seven pounds in man: after substantially complete inhibition of growth the rat made a gain equivalent to an increase in height of eight inches for a man.[2]

The growth and development of creatures whose bodily temperature varies with the temperature of their surroundings may be regulated by temperature control. Tadpoles may be kept at the same stage of development for long periods in an ice-box. The age in days of a tadpole or other cold-blood creature is of no significance whatever in describing its state of development unless temperature is taken into account. The chemical changes involved in assimilation

[1] Osborn, Mendel and Ferry, *Feeding Experiments with Isolated Food Substance*, Washington, 1911, vol. ii, pp. 59-103.

[2] *Ibid.*

and growth may be inhibited more or less indefinitely at low temperatures.[1]

General health conditions in children modify their rate of growing; infection, digestive disturbances and other circumstances have a marked effect. Boston school-boys of nine years of age, for instance, grow only three-quarters of a pound on the average while confined to school from January to June, while during the rest of the year, from June to November, when not confined, they gain three and three-quarter pounds. There are many factors that must be taken into account in this case: in summer there is greater muscular activity; more freedom from bacterial infection, particularly of the respiratory tract; less emotional tension resulting from discipline, competition and enforced association; less mental effort; greater privacy; more abundant ultra-violet light—the effect of these and other factors have yet to be evaluated.[2]

Growth then, and rate of growth, are not " natural " or inscrutable matters — in animals, in plants or in human populations.

Both the increase of populations and the growth of individuals are the net result of *reproduction*—and dissolution; they are essentially similar processes. The growth of individual organisms can be controlled. If we are to discover whether the size of populations may be regulated with a degree of nicety sufficient to assure the effectiveness of a definite population program, we must examine modes of reproduction.

Reproduction is the process by which new life develops from pre-existing life, and by virtue of which animal and plant life continue their existence. An organism continues to grow until it reaches maturity, further growth as an

[1] Minot, C. S., *Age, Growth and Death*, New York, 1908, pp. 88-89.
[2] *Op. cit.*, chapter iii.

individual being impossible it reproduces itself, and so to speak continues growth in its offspring.

" Growth," says Cokkinis,[1] " is but one part of the cycle of reproduction." It is equally true that reproduction is but one part of the process of growth. Reproduction always necessitates the fragmentation of existing organisms, the splitting off of a reproductive fragment from the parent.[2] It is half of the life cycle. The other half is the development of the reproductive fragment to an adult by the process of growth.

There are two methods of reproduction. In the more ancient method only one parent is concerned. With the more advanced method, offspring result from the cooperation of two parents. This second mode of reproduction has been called *sexual*. The first is called non-sexual or asexual.

In the animal kingdom, asexual reproduction does not occur except among the lowest orders; there, reproduction is by simple fragmentation—in one of three forms: fission, budding, spore formation.

Reproduction by equal division is exemplified in the amoebae, one-celled animals, microscopic drops of living jelly (protoplasm) possessing a nucleus. The nucleus divides; the halves migrate away from each other; the containing body takes on a dumb-bell shape (with one-half of the nucleus in each lobe); fission follows. Very simple — in rough outline—but very intricate and subtile when grasped one button lower. This elementary mode of reproduction expresses two striking facts: in producing offspring the parent is destroyed; but the parent finds immortality in offspring—though this last is true merely in principle, for in a frightful number of instances adverse happenings de-

---

[1] *The Reproduction of Life*, New York, 1926, p. 67.

[2] Woodruff, A. A., *Foundations of Biology*, New York, 1922, p. 17.

stroy forever these tiny life forms. Only the main life stream is immortal.

Among unicellulars, the rate of increase is beyond belief. Beginning with a tiniest mass, there is apparently no limit to the amount of protoplasm that may be obtained by the process of division. Assuming a new generation each hour—and many unicellulars exceed that rate—the descendants of a single individual would exceed, before the end of the first day, 10,000,000. It has been said of one microscopic organism that, given a culture medium in which growth and reproduction could proceed unhindered, its descendants would in a month become sufficiently numerous to form a mass a million times larger than the sun.[1] Such reproductive powers leave no room for any trace of doubt that among the unicellulars, population size is determined by death rates: ruthless, sweeping destruction gobbles up these micro-organisms almost as rapidly as they reproduce. Blindly, frantically they multiply, struggle, and are destroyed.

Budding, a second mode of reproduction among unicellulars, means—as the word implies—reproduction by unequal division.

Under conditions unfavorable to life, most bacteria have the trick of reproducing by the formation of spores: a process of multiple fission. Spores are very tough and persistent structures. It may require sixty minutes immersion in boiling water to destroy spores—whereas bacteria are destroyed by a five-minute immersion. Life has two general aspects: one of incredible fragility, one of incredible persistence.

Higher forms of animal life reproduce by the sexual method: two parents cooperate to produce offspring. The essential difference between parents lies in the reproductive fragments they produce. The reproductive fragments of

[1] Reuter, E. B., *Population Problems*, Philadelphia, 1923, p. 112.

sexed organisms are invariably single cells which are almost if not entirely free and independent. The male cell is known as the *sperm*, and the female as the *ovum*.

But to return for a moment to the simpler and far more ancient asexual method of reproduction by division: *Paramecium* is a one-celled animal but a far higher development than the amoeba.

As a rule, reproduction is by equal division, but if external conditions are unfavorable, Paramecium apparently becomes too weak to reproduce alone. Two of these tiny animals approach one another and unite in the region of the mouth; their protoplasm (the material of their bodies) becomes continuous through a connecting bridge which forms between them. A tiniest fragment from each animal, representing the male element, passes over the connecting bridge into the body of the other animal and there unites with a female fragment. The two animals separate and appear to be greatly strengthened and refreshed by this act of union, for they are thenceforth able to produce healthy offspring. Here one undoubtedly witnesses something very like the dawn of sex.[1]

It appears that Paramecium indulges in coition only when its vitality is depressed. This then is the meaning of sex in life, a revitalizing process, which however is concerned almost entirely with the production of vigorous offspring— rather than with welfare of parents.

As one runs up the scale of animal development sex appears to play an increasingly significant part in life. Among the highest species of animals, sex, its attributes and consequences dominate life so completely that even the innate desire to preserve self seems often to be entirely submerged.[2]

[1] Woodruff, A. A., *Foundations of Biology*, New York, 1922, pp. 39, 41, 212, 213, 244-247.

[2] Cokkinis, A. J., *The Reproduction of Life*, pp. 77-78.

In the lowest orders of the animal kingdom the sex instinct does not go beyond coition, or the act of sexual union, but with the higher orders, especially with birds and mammals, the sex instinct expresses itself before, and long after, coition—in courting, in homebuilding, in hatching, in feeding and protecting the young, in reciprocal assistance between parents, and in other ways.

Although the prolificness of even the lower multicellular animals does not approach the horrific reproduction rates of the unicellulars, their rapidity of multiplication indicates almost incredible over-propagation. The average female oyster (of the Maryland variety), for example, lays about 16,000,000 eggs each season. If one-half of these developed into female oysters and reproduced at the same rate, there would be in the second season 64,000,000,000,000 grandchildren of that one female oyster. Great-grandchildren would number 512,000,000,000,000,000. The fifth generation would amount to 66,000,000,000,000,000,000,000,000,000, 000,000,000 oysters. Here it is assumed that but one batch of eggs is laid by each female: actually, they live for years and produce a brood with every season. Allowing eight cubic inches as the amount of space occupied by an oyster, fifth-generation descendants of one female oyster would constitute a mass eight times as large as the earth.[1]

The lowest vertebrate is the fish. Its reproductive rate is large; but fish do not multiply as rapidly as the species just discussed. The behavior of one fish, however, commands especial attention because it illustrates male care, which is so effective in increasing survival rates among offspring in higher species. The male *Stickleback* furnishes the greater share of labor in preparing shelter and in caring for offspring. As mating time approaches, he builds on the bottom of the brook a nest of weeds, stones and random materials;

---

[1] Brooks, W. K., *The Oyster*, Baltimore, 1891, pp. 10 *et seq.*

he then devotes himself to one or more females, whom he entices or drives into his nest. There the female deposits her ova, and he fertilizes them. Diligently the male stickle-back guards his nest until the young appear and become strong enough to fend for themselves and swim away. Reviewing the entire array of animal species, it is not until one comes to the very highest that the male is found devoting anything like this amount of energy and attention to the perpetuation of his kind. Only among members of the human species is an equal degree of paternal care witnessed.[1]

The essential features of reproduction among birds (the lowest of the warm-blooded vertebrates) are familiar to everyone. Prolificness is not as great as among species that take on the temperature of their surroundings, but multiplication goes on at a rate astounding to anyone who has not made a careful study of reproduction. Robins produce from one to three broods annually. To be well within the mark, the yearly increase of each pair of robins may be set at four. The second season there would be four more robins from the original pair and the four produced the first year would beget eight, a total of eighteen robins at the end of the second season. Continuing this rate of increase for ten years the descendants of the original pair of robins would exceed one hundred thousand. By the end of the twentieth year they would exceed twenty billion.[2]

In its anatomy and mode of reproduction the rabbit typifies the mammalian class so well that it can serve as an illustration for the entire order. Rabbits mate about four times a year—in spring and summer months. During these seasons the female produces ripened ova with each lunar period. There are six to eight young in a litter, and about four

[1] Cokkinis, A. J., *op. cit.*, pp. 172-173.
[2] Reuter, E. B., *Population Problems*, Philadelphia, 1923, pp. 113-114.

litters appear each year. Thus a female rabbit may rear
some thirty offspring annually. In the fifth generation, descendants of a single pair should number 2048; in the tenth
generation 2,097,052; and in the fifteenth generation, that
is, in less than four years, the family of one pair of rabbits
should number 4,294,672,496. The rabbit is a comparatively defenseless animal with many enemies. Its rapid rate
of reproduction, principally, saves it from extinction. (*But
this condition, as we are coming to see, is true in great or
less degree of all life forms.*)

It may be objected that a notoriously rapid breeder, the
rabbit, is not a fair example of the mammalian class; but a
pair of even the slowest known breeders, elephants, would
in the course of 745 years produce a progeny of 19,000,000.[1]

Throughout this outline of animal reproduction, one thing
stands out sharp, clear, irrefragable: the size of animal
populations is determined solely by death rates; power of
reproduction, fecundity, is such that any species, if fed and
protected from violence and disease, would soon inundate
the world with its like. Nature reproduces wantonly and
kills ruthlessly—everywhere. Species persist mainly through
the steam-roller effect of incredible prolificness. Weapons of
offense and defense, teeth, claws, horns, shells and hair, all
help — as does intelligence — but that minimum degree of
progress essential to survival is the result of overpropa-
gation.

According to Spencer the prolificness of a species is in
direct proportion to its helplessness.[2] But man, one of the
most defenseless of animals, has persisted in the struggle to
live and has finally prevailed over all other kinds, not by
over-propagation alone, but also by intelligence. In later

[1] Darwin, Charles, *Origin of Species*, London, 1885, p. 52.

[2] Spencer, H., *Principles of Biology*, New York, 1897, vol. ii, pp.
410-413.

chapters it will appear that man is coming to depend more and more on intelligence for both security and progress— and constantly less upon prolificness.

Among animals, reproduction is an automatic process. The mode of growth of individuals and the mode of animal increase are strikingly similar. Man, however, is capable of reflective thinking. Since man is today able to control to a remarkable extent the obscure and subtle process of growth, it is obvious that he may control the rate of human increase as easily as one can regulate the flow of water from a tap.

CHAPTER IX

The Biology of Population Growth

In remotest times man lived, reproduced and died precisely as did other kinds. But recent millenniums have brought a new element into the mode of human increase—an element derived from mankind's most distinctive characteristics. Man is capable of conceptual thought and reflective thinking. He forms free ideas. He talks; he writes; he acts upon tradition. Among other animals, in some slight sense, experience is transmitted from one generation to another; to that extent these animals are aided by tradition. Relatively, however, tradition is so insignificant among the lower animals that for the moment it may be regarded as exclusively a human character. These psychologic and social characters, conceptual thought, reflective thinking and tradition affect population growth profoundly and cause it to differ sharply from the mode of animal increase.

It is apparent everywhere that child-producing capacity, or fecundity, and the number of children that mature are very different matter. It is equally apparent, when first-rate scholars use the terms *fecundity, fertility* and *birth rate* in the same or similar connections, that a definite population terminology is needed. Throughout this work *fecundity* will mean propagating capacity. *Fertility* will mean in every case the actual gross rate of human increase: in general, it will be taken to have the same meaning as birth rate, the number of live births per thousand inhabitants, though it would be slightly more satisfactory to use *fertility* in the more precise sense of the number of live births per hundred women of child-bearing age. However, *birth rate,* which is the more familiar term, and *fecundity* will be used as far as possible to the exclusion of all other terms. The important point to remember is that *capacity* to produce offspring, that is, the maximum rate at which offspring can be produced, will always be called *fecundity.*

Differences in fecundity are extremely difficult or impossible to ascertain. The reactions of tradition, public opinion, and the spontaneous ideas of individuals have created such wide and indefinite differences between fecundity and the actual number of births that it is impossible to find even in the back waters of humanity offspring produced at rates that represent full capacity. Furthermore, when a difference in fecundity is detected with a reasonable degree of certainty, it is extremely difficult to say whether that difference is the result of racial, environmental, or individual variations. We shall nevertheless recite the evidence and see if we can detect constants or trends that will help us to ascertain the mode of human increase.

In order to determine as closely as possible the facts of human reproduction in a state of nature, one must turn to the earliest pages of history and to authoritative opinion concerning pre-historic man. Scant though these data are, they can be eked out to an extent by inference from facts observed among extremely primitive modern peoples and tribes.

Since the male ejects some 226,000,000 sperms with each completed sexual act, and since what the Reverend T. R. Malthus calls the passion between the sexes is such as to insure coition far more frequently than necessary to reproduce a constant state of pregnancy, we may confine entirely to the female our attempt to estimate human fecundity.[1]

---

[1] Pearl, Raymond, *The Biology of Population Growth,* New York, 1925, pp. 179-204.

In determining — as far as possible — the direction and extent of change in fecundity between modern civilized man and man existing in a state of nature, attention may be given first to total sterility. One out of six marriages in the United States produce no offspring.[1] The extent to which this is voluntary or involuntary is not of course determinable. However, the fact that childlessness is more than twice as frequent among native as among foreign-born women suggests that it is in large part voluntary.[2]

Sterility may be congenital or acquired. It has been determined with reasonable certainty that at least one-third of all sterile marriages are the fault of the male.[3] There is no critical evidence of variation in congenital sterility from one epoch to another, but since acquired sterility is nearly always the result of disease, there is reason to believe that there has been at least some slight increase in total sterility, for it seems that disease is a comparatively modern phenomenon. This last point, however, must not be labored too hard, for evidences of disease are found upon very early human remains. Furthermore, during the first and second quarters of the twentieth century several diseases were made almost obsolete. It is probable that, considering the whole world around, disease reached its highest effectiveness in suppressing the growth of population during the Middle Ages—and this, quite likely, applies to the special case of sterility.[4] Sterility is not uncommon among modern primitive peoples, and it is fair to infer from this fact and from ancient lore that it was prevalent in the same degree among

[1] *Statistical Bulletin*, Metropolitan Life Insurance Co., December, 1927.
[2] *Loc. cit.*
[3] Carr-Saunders, A. M., *The Population Problem*, London, 1922, p. 89.
[4] *Cf.* East, E. M., *Mankind at the Crossroads*, New York, 1923, pp. 261-262.

prehistoric peoples.[1] The large probability is that positive, irremediable sterility is less prevalent today than at any earlier time.

Menstruation, though not directly pertinent, has some bearing upon the mode of human increase. It is perhaps not too much to say that the fundamental, biologic factors in population growth and menstruation are affected in precisely the same way by heredity, race, climate, comfort and feeding. If menstruation is not greatly affected by climate (at least not in any immediate sense) neither is population growth. If, on the other hand, menstruation is affected by other environmental differences (for example, the degree of ease in living conditions), it is possible that fecundity and human increase are similarly affected. Englemann gives the following figures:[2]

Climatic Zone	Menstruation Begins At:
Cold	16.5 years
Temperate	15.5 "
Tropics	12.9 "

Krieger does not differ significantly:[3]

Place	Menstruation Begins At:					
Christiania	16	years	9	months	25	days
Berlin	15	"	7	"	25	"
London	15	"	1	"	14	"
Lyons	14	"	5	"	29	"
Marseilles	13	"	11	"	11	"
Calcutta	12	"	6	"	0	"
Sierra Leone	10	"	0	"	0	"

On further examination it appears, however, that menstruation is far more a matter of race than of climate—

[1] *Cf.* Duncan, H. G., *Race and Population Problems*, New York, 1929, pp. 264-265.

[2] Englemann, G. J., *Trans. Amer. Gyn Soc.*, vol. xxvi, p. 87.

[3] Krieger, E., *Die Menstruation*, Berlin, 1869.

assuming, of course, a uniform state of welfare. Merely, it happens that the races of the world remain, in spite of improved transportation and consequent greater migration, distributed roughly according to climate. In the United States however — a " new " country — where population is extremely mixed and where at least a few representatives of most races are found in every climate zone, and where the country extends from the 29th to the 45th parallel of northern latitude, and the annual average temperature ranges from 40° F. to 70° F., it appears that the age at which menstruation begins differs only from race to race without regard to climate.

There is definite evidence that menstruation, and perhaps by fair inference the whole biologic foundation of the population problem in all of its details and implications, is almost solely a matter of race. A great variety of races exist in Hungary. Krieger reports the following figures, taken from Joachim: [1]

Race	Average Age at which Menstruation Begins
Slavonic	16–17 years
Magyar	15–16 "
Jewish	14–15 "
Styrian	13–14 "

Race is a product of climate and other elements of environment. That is to say, in earliest times high surrounding mountains or other barriers pocketed people in certain regions; breeding down through the centuries, these people gradually took on mental and physical traits adapted to success in that region. Among scientifically-minded persons it is difficult to maintain other hypotheses of race.

A matter of great import in drawing a suggestive outline of the mode of population growth is the fact that the beginning of menstruation varies notably with differences in

[1] Krieger, *op. cit.*

living conditions. Krieger gives the following figures:[1]

EFFECT OF ECONOMIC STATUS UPON BEGINNING OF MENSTRUATION

	Brienne de Boisoment		Tilt		Krieger		Rain	
	Years	Months	Years	Months	Years	Months	Years	Months
Upper Class ...	13	8	13	5½	14	1⅙	14	3
Middle Class ..	14	5	14	3½	14	4⅗	15	5½
Lower Class ...	14	1	..	..	16	8⅕	16	5¼

Krieger also reports that Mayer found the average age at which menstruation begins among women of the upper classes to be 14.69 years and among poor women 16.0 years. Furthermore, good living conditions prolong the period during which women are capable of bearing children. Menstruation comes to an end sooner among laboring than among wealthier classes.[2]

It has been frequently observed that animals brought into captivity experience a change in sexual seasons. Animals that are intense, passionate, violent, in general the carnivore, become disorganized in some indefinite way — possibly, an emotional matter—and there is a falling-off or total loss of fecundity. In many more cases, however, there is a gain in fertility and probably in fecundity. Perhaps it is not going too far to infer that if the easier living conditions of captivity usually produce increased fecundity in wild animals, man, in climbing upward through the ages, reaching at last the comparative ease of modern civilization, has gained in fecundity.[3]

[1] *Op. cit.*

[2] Marshall, F. H. A., *Physiology of Reproduction* (2nd and rev. ed.), London, 1922.

[3] *Cf. Report World Population Conference*, London, 1927 (Crew, F. A. E.), pp. 218, 219.

The wild dog of South America, the wolf, and the fox breed but once a year under natural conditions; in captivity they experience two annual heats—like the domestic dog.[1] The otter, in a state of nature, breeds but once a year; in captivity an oestrum may occur regularly at monthly intervals the year round. Annually, under natural conditions, the red deer goes through two oestrums of three weeks each, but in captivity the sexual season extends over the entire year.[2] Marshall says, " There is every reason for supposing that the processes of growth and menstruation can be very largely influenced both by sufficiency of food supply on the one hand and by artificial stimulations on the other." [3]

The number of young in each litter is greater among animals enjoying an easy, domesticated life than among their wild cousins. The wild rabbit is said to produce six young at a time: litters from tame rabbits vary from four to eleven, and in one well-known case, eighteen, all of which lived.[4] The wild sow bears from five to eight young at each conception—sometimes twelve. A domestic sow that produces a litter of less than eight is held in slight esteem by breeders. A conspicuous feature common to the life of domesticated species and civilized man — in contrast with species in a state of nature—is the increase in the richness and regularity of their diet; other living conditions are much improved. Better food and generally improved conditions of living increase the life span, lengthen the period of fecundity in women, increase the size of litters among lower animals and speed up the oestrus cycle.[5] Well-fed and

[1] Marshall, *op. cit.*, p. 57.

[2] Carr-Saunders, A. M., *The Population Problem*, London, 1922.

[3] Marshall, *op. cit.*, p. 595.

[4] Darwin, Charles, *Variations of Animals and Plants under Domestication*, vol. ii, p. 90.

[5] *Cf. Nature*, v. 122: 136-8.

well-cared-for animals are more fecund, it appears, than their feral cousins—Adam Smith's " half-starved Highland woman who frequently bears more than twenty children " to the contrary notwithstanding![1]

Another point of evidence is presented in the matter of twins. Among modern civilized men twins occur about once in ninety births.[2] According to Duncan, the rate is one in eighty births.[3] Throughout the entire Hebrew Scripture, where so much attention is given to fecundity, fertility and prolificity, twins are scarcely mentioned; and among all very ancient peoples the appearance of twins was a rare and momentous matter.

All evidence points to one conclusion. *If there has been any change in fecundity in the course of human history, it has been in the direction of increase.*[4] Professor Ross' opinion is that, " We reject the cheering argument of Herbert Spencer that civilization begets individuation and that, as individuation progresses, reproductive power declines. The fact is, the women of the most civilized peoples, if anything, are more fruitful than those of the less advanced." [5] Charles Darwin writes: " There is reason to suspect that the reproductive power is actually less in barbarians than in civilized races. It is highly probable that savages, who suffer much more hardship and do not obtain so much nutritious food as civilized men, would be actually less prolific." [6]   And Heape says:

[1] *Wealth of Nation*, bk. i, chap. viii.

[2] For New York City the rate was: in 1926, 0.8281; in 1927, 0.9108; in 1928, 0.9595. (Frequency of twins per hundred births.)

[3] Duncan, J. M., *Fecundity, Fertility and Sterility, Edinburgh*, 1871, p. 67.

[4] *Birth Rate Commission* (British), First Report, *passim*; also East, E. M., *Mankind at the Crossroads*, New York, 1923, p. 258.

[5] Ross, E. A., *Scientific Monthly*, 24: 266.

[6] Darwin, Charles, *Descent of Man*, London, 1871, p. 132. For a view that modifies somewhat this statement see C. Gini, *Proceedings of the Conference*, London, 1927, pp. 165-167.

It would seem highly probable that the reproductive power of mankind has increased with civilization, precisely as it has been increased in the lower animals by domestication; that the effect of a regular supply of good food, together with all the other stimulating factors available and exercised in modern civilized communities has resulted in such great activity of the generative organs, and so great an increase in the supply of the reproductive elements, that conception in the healthy human female may be said to be possible almost at any time during the reproductive period.[1]

Among animals, the human female is the only one that receives the male at any time. Formerly it was believed that among civilized human beings conception could follow copulation upon any of the three hundred and sixty-five days in a year. It appears, however, that during the World War married German soldiers were not given leave of absence except upon occasion, and then only for two or three days at a time; therefore it was possible to determine the period in the sexual cycle at which some two or three hundred babies were conceived. From these data Siegel concluded that the likelihood of fertilization increases from the beginning of menstruation, reaches the highest point six days later, remains at nearly the same height until the twelfth or thirteenth day and then declines until the twenty-second day, after which there is absolute sterility.[2] If these data are confirmed, the ancient custom which encouraged copulation immediately after menstruation among Hebrews and discouraged it among the Hindus, is definitely pertinent in a population study. After more thorough consideration, however, Siegel concluded that there remains some slight doubt as to the universal reliability of the " safe period," and other authorities concur.[3]

[1] Quoted by Carr-Saunders, *op. cit.*, p. 101.

[2] *Munchener Medizinische Wochenschrift*, 1916, p. 718.

[3] Siegel, P. W., *Gewollte und Ungewollte Schwankungen der Weiblichen Fructbarkeit*, Berlin, 1917; *cf.* Haire, N., *Some More Medical Views on Birth Control*, New York, 1928, p. 12 and *passim*.

A simple exercise in numbers will illustrate the power of human fecundity which, as we have seen, is constantly underestimated. Consider a population of 1,000,000 born in the same year, half of whom are males and half females. Let us suppose that all marry, and that each couple, before the age of twenty, produces two children, a boy and a girl. For the sake of simplicity, imagine that at the end of each twenty-year period, parents die simultaneously with the birth of their offspring. Then, if the children marry and produce offspring as did their parents, we shall have a *stationary* population of 1,000,000. If, however, the average number of children is two and one-half per couple, in one hundred years the population will amount to 3,050,000; if three children, 7,954,000; if four, 32,000,000; if five, 97,650,000.

Dublin, in discussing the number of children that must be born on the average per family to assure a stationary population in the United States, says that quite obviously each thousand females must bear a thousand daughters if the population is to remain stationary. As a matter of fact, however, a considerable number will die without bearing daughters. Thus, the burden of bearing one thousand daughters will fall upon a fraction of the original thousand females. Under mortality and marital conditions prevailing in 1920, he found that of every thousand females born, 788 eventually marry. Consequently in each generation 788 married women must give birth to a thousand daughters. To put it another way, each thousand married women to replace their number must rear 1,268 daughters.

Likewise, making due allowance for boys who die in infancy or childhood and those who do not marry, 742 men must beget one thousand sons; which is to say, each thousand married men must produce 1,350 sons.

Combining the figures, it appears that each thousand

families to replace their numbers must rear 1,268 daughters and 1,350 sons—an average for each family of 2.6 children.

There are many marriages, however — probably one in six—that do not result in children. The burden of child-bearing consequently falls on the other five-sixths; these families must therefore bring into the world not an average of 2.6, but 3.1 children.

Dublin says of the result of his calculations:

It will be a source of surprise to many that the figure we have obtained is so large. It is, however, less than a calculation made on the basis of the 1910 figures. Under the mortality conditions prevailing at that time, the average number of children per fertile family necessary to maintain a stationary population, was 3.3. The difference of about one-fifth of a birth, or one birth for five fruitful marriages, represents a saving resulting primarily from the lowered death rate and especially the infant mortality rate.[1]

In a group of 1,007 married women over forty-five years of age Dublin found the actual number of children born averaged 3.7.

The power of population to increase finds apt illustration in the French population of Canada. In 1920 French Canadians numbered more than three million. History reveals that substantially all of them were the descendants of 5800 settlers who arrived before 1680.[2] Leroy-Beaulieu puts it this way: When Canada was lost to France in 1763, the French population amounted to 65,000; by 1901 it had grown to 1,649,371. And then he reminds us that even this prodigious increase required a *rate* of increase far less than the Malthusian, the classic and frequently exceeded, rate of doubling every twenty-five years. Had the French

[1] *Statistical Bulletin*, Metropolitan Life Insurance Co., New York, December, 1924.

[2] Ross, E. A., *Standing Room Only?*, New York, 1927, p. 85.

population of Canada doubled every twenty-five years it would have amounted to more than 3,000,000 in 1911.[1]

The population of Europe at the beginning of the eighteenth century was 90,000,000;[2] by the middle of the century it had reached, according to Wilcox, 127,000,000.[3] Levasseur's estimate for the close of the century was 180,000,000. By 1916 Europe's population had grown to 465,000,000. Moreover, during the preceding century Europe poured out her blood over the entire globe, especially in America, Australia and Africa; in 1916 the descendants of this outpouring numbered 185,000,000. Therefore, persons of European ancestry amounted, at that time, to 650,000,000—a threefold increase in numbers in little more than a century.[4]

The estimate of Knibbs (1928) for the rate of population growth in certain countries follow:[5]

RATE OF POPULATION GROWTH IN CERTAIN COUNTRIES

Country	Rate Per 1,000	Years to Double
France	1.6	436
Norway	6.6	105
Sweden	8.4	83
Austria-Hungary	8.5	82
Spain	8.7	80
England	10.4	67
Japan	10.8	64
Holland	12.2	57
Germany	13.6	51
Rumania	14.8	47
United States	18.2	38
Australia	20.3	34
Canada	29.3	24

[1] Leroy-Beaulieu, P., *La Question de la Population*, p. 130.

[2] Levasseur, P., *La Population Francaise*, Paris, 1889-1892.

[3] *American Economic Review*, vol. v, pp. 741-742.

[4] Rossiter, W. S., *Journal of the American Statistical Association*, March, 1923; East, E. M., *Mankind at the Cross Roads*, New York, 1923, p. 77.

[5] Knibbs, Sir George, *The Shadow of the World's Future*, London, 1928, p. 47.

Taking even the comparatively microscopic French rate of increase, the present population of the world could have been produced by a single couple had they begun 11,000 years ago.

Let us quote Henry George on hypothetical fertility:

For the solitary example of a family that has survived any great lapse of time, even though assured of subsistence and honor, we must go to unchangeable China. The descendants of Confucius still exist there, and enjoy peculiar privileges and consideration, forming, in fact, the only hereditary aristocracy. On the presumption that population tends to double every twenty-five years, they should, in 2,150 years after the death of Confucius have amounted to 859,559,193,106,709,672,198,710,-528 souls.[1]

But all this is merely so much mathematics; and population growth is a matter of biology, economics, psychology. Furthermore, Malthus summed it up a century and a half ago when he said: " The actual rate of increase is extremely slow, while power to increase is prodigious." [2]

The circumstance which checks directly the " prodigious " power of increase in all life forms is, of course, wealth (weal); those items of well-being that exist under scarcity conditions. Most of the material presented in the last four chapters has added to the substance of the first clause of our formula: populations tend to increase as wealth increases. From much of the material examined, especially sociological material, there appeared some slight evidential confirmation of the second clause of our hypothesis: populations tend to decrease as living standards rise—but more of that in later chapters.

We must turn now from a very general study of life and

[1] George, Henry, *Progress and Poverty*, New York, 1899, pp. 111-12.

[2] Article: *Population*, MacVey Napier Supp. to Encyclo. Brit., 1824.

its circumstances—especially of human life and its environment — to a particular study of the immediate influences
controlling the net rate of human increase: birth rates and
death rates.   The interest of most students of population
growth stops with death rates and birth rates.   Ours does
not: our greatest concern is with the *forces that govern*
birth rates and death rates.   To uncover these forces a careful examination must be made of all available data.   But to
one force or influence which has some slight bearing upon
death rates and birth rates, immigration, a separate chapter
will be accorded.

CHAPTER X

DEATH RATES

DECREASED death rates explain all marked gains in modern populations. Nowhere have birth rates increased—except in very small areas or during very short periods of time.[1]

It is difficult to say just what death rates were in prehistoric times, or even to be certain that they were larger or smaller than in recent years. A scanning of the evidence might lead to the conclusion that death rates were in earliest time extremely high—higher than in any subsequent period; but that view is not fully warranted. Disease was not nearly so general as in a later day and the death rate from disease was in consequence much lower; disease probably reached its greatest force as a life-destroying power in the middle ages. The death rate from accident and violence of one sort or another was probably much higher in pre-historic than in mediæval or in modern times. Intelligence flowed at a slightly — very slightly — lower level, while ferocious beasts everywhere destroyed all but the quickest, strongest, and most intelligent of mankind. Wars and feuds were frequent, relentless, devastating.

It seems, therefore, that although death rates from disease were lower, death rates from accident and violence counteracted that benefit, and death rates, in general, were probably higher than at any subsequent time — though undoubtedly there were fairly large population groups, which, during the

[1] East, E. M., *Mankind at the Crossroads*, New York, 1923, p. 271.

middle ages suffered far heavier losses from plague and war than man experienced at any date, earlier or later.

Nearly all of these conclusions concerning death rates among prehistoric peoples are of course derived to a great extent from observation of death rates among extremely primitive contemporary peoples.

In the same way it may be inferred from observation of modern primitives that infant mortality rates in earliest days were frightful.[1]   Modern primitives are extremely casual in their treatment of infants; extremely ignorant, judged by modern standards and experience.   In ancient times, with no apparatus, prepared foods or animal milk, the risk of death during the first months of life was large. On the African west coast, it is said that nine out of every ten babies die during the first months of life.   In certain provinces of China, it is estimated that seventy-five to eighty-five per cent of all children born die during early infancy.[2]   Returns from Hongkong, in 1909, showed the number of deaths of children under one year of age to be eighty per cent of the number of births.[3]   In Bombay, during the five-year period ending 1922, every second child died before the end of the first year.[4]

So common was the death of an infant in earliest times that no one cared to waste time rearing any but the most promising.   Several tribes of modern primitives dip new-born children into cold water and expose them to other

[1] " The infant death rate is usually expressed as a certain number of deaths under one year of age per thousand born during the particular year." Chaddock, R. E., *Principles and Methods of Statistics*, New York, 1925, p. 30.

[2] *Second Report of the British Birth Rate Commission*, 1920, pp. 317.

[3] Ross, E. A., *The Changing Chinese*, New York, 1911, p. 103.

[4] Das, T., *Religions and Ethical Aspects of Birth Control* (M. Sanger, ed.), New York, 1925, p. 205.

rigorous tests which eliminate large numbers. Such practices in themselves necessarily aggravate infant mortality, and it is quite possible that the African west coast rate was nearly universal in earliest times; only one of every ten babies survived the early months of life. Lord Astor reminds us that in John Wesley's time less than twenty-five in every hundred children lived to see a fifth birthday.[1] There was in all probability a constant improvement in the general death rate after the middle ages, but it was not until almost the beginning of the twentieth century that a sharp downward trend was given to infant mortality rates.[2]

The modern range of infant mortality rates is wide. It is therefore impossible to give general or characteristic figures. Infant mortality rates vary not only between different temperature zones, different cultural areas, different nations, localities and cities, but between various social, educational, and economic classes within the same region.[3]

In the Western civilization, infant mortality rates appear to be lowest in Scandinavian countries and in the British colonies, especially in New Zealand and Australia. Infant mortality rates appear to be highest in eastern Europe and in the north, west, and extreme south of South America. In the most enlightened regions of the earth about sixty out of every thousand infants die during the first year, whereas in the more backward countries of Western civilization the rate often rises as high as three hundred deaths per thousand live births—or even more.[4] Among less civilized or savage

---

[1] *The Round Table*, No. 72 (Sept., 1928), "The Birth Rate and the British Commonwealth," p. 779.

[2] Kuczynski, R. R., *The Balance of Births and Deaths*, New York, 1928, p. 49.

[3] U. S. Dept. of Labor, B. P. No. 9, *Infant Mortality*.

[4] U. S. Dept. of Labor, B. P. No. 105, *Infant Mortality, etc. in New Zealand*.

peoples infant mortality rates are of course far higher. Even within one country, as for example the United States, the rate varies widely.[1] In nearly all regions of the earth, however civilized, infant mortality rates might, with the application of well-known methods of caring for infants, be made markedly lower.[2]

Certain backward communities in the United States do not as yet record deaths and births. In fact, at the time of the World War, when the draft act went into effect and a great many persons were anxious to prove that they were— or were not—of military age, a large number were embarrassed to find that what to them was the most important event of all time, their birth, had not been noted.[3] Indeed, scarcely more than half the population of the United States lived at that time within areas that recorded births; and not quite four-fifths lived within areas where deaths were recorded. This situation has been much improved.

Infant mortality in the birth-registration area of the United States varied in 1927 from the extreme, high rate of 130.1 (possibly an error) in Arizona to 49.7 in the state of Washington. The next highest infant mortality rate (after Arizona's, just given) is Maryland's, 81.5.[4]

It is natural to suppose that the highest mortality rates should be found in states having a large foreign-born population, where ignorance presumably runs at a high level, and where civilization presumably does not—or perhaps in states

[1] U. S. Dept. of Commerce *Infant Mortality Statistics* for 1926, Government Printing Office, Washington, 1929.

[2] American Pub. Health Association, *Health Officers' News Letter*, vol. iv, no. 11; East, E. M., *op. cit.*, pp. 344-347.

[3] U. S. Dept. of Commerce, *Mortality Statistics: 1926*, Washington, 1929, p. 10.

[4] Dept. of Commerce, *Photo-stat of Current Records*, Jan., 1929. Possession of author.

having an extremely large proportion of negroes in their population. South Carolina and Mississippi are the only states in which more than half the population is made up of negroes; Alabama, Georgia, and Louisiana have the next largest negro admixture. States having the largest proportion of foreign-born residents are New York, Massachusetts, Connecticut, and Rhode Island. The highest infant mortality rates, however, are found in Maryland (81.5) and in Maine (80.0), states which have neither an extremely high proportion of foreign-born nor of colored persons in their populations—indeed these two states have in their populations as large a proportion of descendants of colonial stock as any two states in the Union. On the other hand, states having low infant death rates, and where presumably civilization and enlightenment have reached high levels are Washington, Idaho and Nebraska. The state of Washington has a larger proportion of foreign-born residents than has Maine and a much larger proportion than Maryland.

Infant mortality rates among the several states may be said to range roughly from fifty to eighty per thousand—an extremely wide margin, indicating beyond doubt that, with the expenditure of a little more money and effort, the average rate for the United States—in spite of recent improvement—could be made very much lower.[1]

A strong impression of progress is given by a study of recent infant mortality rates in regions well up in, but by no means at the top of, the scale of intelligence in the care of infants. In 1914 the infant mortality rate for England and Wales was 105; by 1918 it had fallen to 97, and in 1927 the rate was 65.[2] The rate in the United States (*Registra-*

---

[1] Newsholme, Sir Arthur, *The Elements of Vital Statistics*, New York, 1924, p. 377.

[2] *Quarterly Return of the Registrar-General for England and Wales* (quarter ended 31st, December, 1928).

tion Area) fell from 86.4 in 1919 to 70.8 in 1924 and to 64.6 in 1927.[1] Although conditions of birth and early rearing have improved more rapidly in England and Wales than in the United States, the American rate shows a marked improvement: in Pennsylvania, for example, infant death rates fell from 167 in 1906 to 114 in 1916, to 82 in 1926, and to 71 in 1929: an average infant has three times as great a chance of surviving its first year as one had twenty-five years ago.[2]

To substantiate the statement that infant mortality rates decrease notably with improved living conditions—whether referred to economic, social, political or educational position—completely satisfying proof is not available, but strongly suggestive evidence can be presented. In New York City the infant death rate on the lower East Side nearly doubles the rate on Park Avenue.[3] In Saginaw, Michigan, the infant mortality rate was found to be 179.5 for infants whose parents were in the lowest earning group; deaths decreased rapidly as earnings increased, reaching a minimum mortality rate of 22.2 for the highest wage class—truly striking, but suggesting perhaps that physical soundness, intelligence and education, which are probably related to earning ability, are as significant as mere economic competence. A similar survey in Waterbury, Connecticut showed the same regular decline in infant mortality as the earnings of parents increased. Deaths among infants in the upper and middle classes in England are exactly half as frequent as among the infants of common laborers.[4] In Paris the rate is said

[1] U. S. Dept. of Commerce, *Births, etc., 1927*, Washington, 1929, p. 6.

[2] Pennsylvania Dept. of Health, *Vital Statistics Bulletin*, vol. v, no. 1, January, 1930.

[3] Report of the Bellevue-Yorkville Health Demonstration, Oct., 1928; Report of East Harlem Health Center, 1928.

[4] *National Birth Rate Commission* (British), First Report, p. 353.

to vary from 151 in the poorest districts to 51 in the richest. Similar facts have been found wherever the matter has been investigated.[1]

Evidence of a direct relationship between living conditions and infant mortality is perhaps more clearly shown by the difference between mortality rates for legitimate and illegitimate children in the same region—for it is probably safe to assume that on the average, living conditions are better for legitimates. In Norway, during the four-year period 1910-14, the mortality rate for infants born out of wedlock was 122; for infants born in wedlock the rate was 62. In New South Wales, in 1916, the figures were 145.9 and 63.9. The annual report of the Registrar-General for England and Wales for 1915 gives an infant mortality rate of 203 per thousand illegitimate births and 105 per thousand legitimate births. In Boston, in 1914, the mortality rate among illegitimate infants was 281 per thousand, and among legitimate infants, 95 per thousand. In Baltimore the rates were 315.5 and 95.9 respectively. In 1913 the Health Officer of the District of Columbia reported the death rate for white children born out of wedlock as 302 and for white children born in wedlock, 79.7. Nevertheless, in recent years, infant mortality rates for illegitimate births have declined quite as rapidly as for legitimate births, that is to say, their relationship remains almost constant.

Did not the ancient and savage idea of dipping new-born infants in cold water and otherwise exposing them to hardship evidence a constructive idea? Nature's method of improving the human stock has always been to weed out the unfit by hardship. Are not humanitarian measures, designed

---

[1] *Cf.* Newsholme, Sir Arthur, *op. cit.*, p. 121; also Hibbs, H. H., "The Influence of Economic and Industrial Conditions on Infant Mortality," *Q. Jl. of Economics*, November, 1915; also U. S. Dept. of Labor, B. P. No. 9, *Infant Mortality*.

to reduce infant mortality rates, merely methods of checking or thwarting natural progress? Although it is not possible to give full evidential proof, the opinion of health experts, medical men and students of vital statistics leans toward the contrary conclusion. These men hold that haphazard methods of birth and rearing result in a damage rate that seriously reduces the average vitality of survivors.[1] Or stated conversely, although proper conditions of birth and rearing will result in the survival of many individuals whose physical endowment would not have permitted survival under natural conditions, this marginal group, on the average, is no worse off physically than the badly damaged marginal group surviving under natural conditions—and the favorable variants in the properly-cared-for group are certainly, on the average, far superior to any equally large group born and reared under substantially natural conditions. Even in this enlightened age, the number of children possessing constitutions, parts, digestive tracts and psyches hopelessly damaged by indifferent conditions of birth and rearing is astounding and pitiful.

Adult death rates have declined fairly steadily since the middle ages, and possibly from the beginning of human history; but until very recent times the decline has been tediously slow. The span of life, however, has not been increased, though careless utterances from high authorities lead to the opposite opinion. The *expectation of life,* which is an entirely different matter, has been greatly increased.[2]

The span of life means the average age at death of, say, the most long-lived one per cent of the population. *Expectation of life* means the number of years which a group of persons of exactly the same age may expect on the average to live. There is no evidence whatever that the life span of

[1] Newsholme, Sir A., *op. cit.,* pp. 350-360.

[2] Dublin, L. I., *Health and Wealth,* New York, 1928, pp. 157, 183.

the exceptionally healthy, careful person has been significantly increased—nor is there any very great prospect of considerable increase. The extreme of natural life is slightly more than one hundred years. It is quite true that the number of persons in public life or in the columns of the newspapers who have run through one hundred years seems to increase. We must allow something, however, for the effect of improved means of communication and expanded news-gathering facilities—and something for the distinction an obscure nonogenarian attains by claiming one hundred years. The success, however, of several biologists in keeping bits of living tissue alive and growing in artificial cultures month after month, year after year, suggests very strongly that there is some slight probability, however remote, of lengthening the life span.[1]

Expectation of life increased sensationally—particularly during the first quarter of the twentieth century—but nearly all of the gain was made during the early years of life.[2]

That twenty years have been added to the average length of human life since public health work began to be actively practised in the early eighties of the last century is true. But this gain can be traced to the reduced mortality of infants and to the cutting down of the unnecessary and preventable deaths of young people from typhoid fever, diptheria, scarlet fever, smallpox and a number of other diseases which, for the most part, affect persons under forty years of age.[3]

Indeed for white males, all of the gain in life expectation was made before the forty-second year, and for negroes before the twenty-eighth year. In Pennsylvania, for example,

[1] East, E. M., *op. cit.*, pp 200-201; Fisk, E. L., *Journal of Physical Education*, Feb., 1929, p. 103.

[2] Fisk, *loc. cit.*

[3] *Statistical Bulletin*, Metropolitan Life Insurance Co., vol. x, no. 10; Dublin, Louis I., *op. cit.*, pp. 157 and 333-334.

the general death rate " under five years of age " decreased sixty-two per cent in less than a generation. For ages five to nineteen years the decrease was forty per cent; for ages twenty to thirty-nine years, twenty-nine per cent; forty to fifty-nine years, ten per cent; and for " sixty years and over " the decrease was only five per cent.[1]

When the expectation of life tables compiled by insurance actuaries in the United States in 1910 are compared with Haley's seventeenth-century Breslau table and with the table which Pearson and McDonell compiled from the mummy records of Roman Egypt, although a steady century-to-century improvement in the expectation of life during youth is apparent, the modern advantage over Roman Egypt is entirely lost by the sixty-ninth year. The advantage that modern man has over his seventeenth-century ancestor is lost by the seventy-ninth year. In fact, the person who today is seventy or eighty years old cannot expect to live longer than one of similar age in Roman Egypt, in seventeenth-century Breslau or eighteenth-century England. The strong probability is that he will not live so long, for the rigorous conditions of life in earlier centuries resulted in the survival only of persons extremely well equipped to struggle against the impacts of life and the relentless flood of time.[2]

Comparisons of ancient and modern tables of life expectation are not quite fair however, for ancient tables are in all cases taken from tombstones or mummy cases, and, be it remembered, the poor left no marks. The older records cover then only a small selective population of the very rich or very prominent—and life and health and death are largely economic matters.[3]

[1] Pennsylvania State Dept. of Health, *Vital Statistics Bulletin*, vol. iv, no. 6 (June, 1929).

[2] Hexter, M. B., *Social Consequences of Business Cycles*, pp. 53-55; Dublin, L. I., *op. cit.*, pp. 340-344.

[3] *Proceedings of the World Population Conference*, 1927, Edward Arnold & Co., London, p. 117.

Heredity is an important influence in determining health and longevity—though it can be said, with as great warrant, that environment is an important influence in determining health and longevity.[1] In New York City the death rate in First Avenue is twice as high as it is a few blocks west and north.[2] Pearson, however, found that from fifty to seventy-five per cent of the general death rate is determined solely by heredity, and to that extent therefore there is slight probability of modification by sanitation, hygiene or medicine. Alexander Graham Bell found that where neither parent lived to be eighty, only 5.3 per cent of their offspring lived to that age; that where only one parent lived to be eighty, 9.18 per cent of their offspring reached or passed the age of eighty; and that where both parents reached or passed their eightieth birthday, 20.6 per cent of their offspring reached that age. It may be fairly stated then that one who desires health and longevity must first of all select sound parents and then take care to be rich.[3]

Death rates are in general correlated with birth rates. The highest death rates are found in Russia and Hungary and Chili, nations in which extremely high birth rates prevail: the lowest death rates are found in New Zealand, Australia, Denmark, Norway, the Netherlands—all of them low birth-rate nations.

Very little significant information can be obtained by comparing death rates for the several states of the United States. As with infant mortality rates, the highest general death rates are found, not in states where there is a large foreign

[1] *Proceedings of the World Population Conference*, 1927, Edward Arnold & Co., London, p. 227.

[2] Report, *Bellevue-Yorkville Health Demonstration*, New York, 1928; also Report, East Harlem Health Center, 1928; also Pearl, R., *The Rate of Living*, New York, 1928, chap. vi.

[3] *Cf.* Holmes, S. J., *Univ. of California Publ'n.*, vol. 31, no. 15, pp. 359-375; Newsholme, *op. cit.*, pp. 107-108.

population nor in states where there is a large negro population, but in states which have a large percentage of original colonial stock: top death rates for 1919 appeared in Maine, Maryland, and Vermont—though there were, in all probability, higher rates in non-registration states. The lowest death rates appeared in Kansas, Minnesota, Washington, and Wisconsin—states having a fairly high proportion of foreign-born residents and second-generation Americans. This occurrence of the high death rates and high infant mortality rates in states containing a large proportion of colonial stock, combined with correspondingly low birth rate that we shall find for this same group in a later chapter suggests that, everywhere in the United States, Anglo-Saxon and Germanic, or Teutonic, stocks are being exhausted.

Dublin found, however, that in a purely foreign-born population death rates were appreciably higher than for second and other generation Americans.[1] It is quite obvious that a foreign population, unable to speak the language, unfamiliar with the institutions and customs of the land in which they are resident, will, other things being equal, have a smaller chance of survival than persons who speak the language of the policeman on the corner, the interne in the hospital, the doctor, the nurse, the door-man in the free clinic. The emotional strain of living in unfamiliar circumstances quite possibly accounts for an appreciable amount of the higher death rate among the foreign born. It is quite possible, therefore, that Mr. Dublin is not wholly correct in his surmise that American immigrants may be of an inferior stock—in spite of the fact that he found death rates higher among certain races in New York than among those same races in their native countries.[2]

In view of the popularity on both sides of the Atlantic

[1] Dublin, L. I., *American Economic Review*, vol. vi, p. 548.
[2] Dublin, L. I., *Scientific Monthly*, 14: 94-104.

of books with a strongly journalistic tone, maintaining that
colored races are rising in numbers and gradually engulfing
the whites and that the day of the white race is in its twilight,
it is interesting to see how American statistics point in this
respect.[1] The writers of these ingenious books have curiously enough overlooked an ideal opportunity for studying
this problem. America, with its mixture of white, black
and red races, living in close association for a considerable
period of time under various climatic and economic conditions, presents an almost perfect field for study. The
gradual engulfing and slow absorption of the red race by the
white in North America is too apparent and well known to
be labored here. What of negroes in the United States?

In 1910 the Census Bureau reported a negro death rate
of 30.2. Negro mortality rates exceeded the white for both
sexes and for every age. In the registration area of the
United States in 1911, the death rate for whites was 13.7
and for colored peoples, very largely negroes, 23.7. That is
to say, in the same areas the death rate for negroes was
nearly twice the white death rate. Negro death rates for
northern cities about equal negro birth rates. A recent large
increase in the number of negroes in northern cities is wholly
the result of migration. In 1924 the Department of Public
Health of New York City gave 26.31 as the death rate for
negroes compared with 13.40 for the entire city—including
of course negroes.[2]

Among young people of the negro race within the registration area of the United States the death rate is about ten
times as high as for whites of the same age.[3] In 1926 the

[1] U. S. Dept. of Commerce, *Mortality Statistics for 1926*, Washington,
1929, p. 7.

[2] *Ibid.*

[3] Here in all fairness it must be recalled however that the death rate
among "young people" (15-20 years) of the white race is almost
negligible.

infant mortality rate, including negroes, was 73—for negroes alone the rate was 112.[1]

It is doubtless true that negroes are less immune than whites to some diseases, but it is also true that they are more immune to others. The principal explanation of the higher negro death rate in all civilized countries seems to lie in the depressed social and economic circumstances of the negro—and in the emotional shocks caused by the mechanism of modern life. The enormously higher death rate for negroes under twenty years of age is quite likely an economic matter.

Data from many parts of the world — principally from Australia, New Zealand, and South America—confirm the conclusions yielded by the facts already cited concerning death rates for white and dark races. Surely, any who doubts the ultimate prevalence of the white race ought to be persuaded to the contrary opinion by the definite, recorded, objective, statistical evidence presented over a period of nearly 150 years in the United States census reports. Here a white and a black race live under as nearly equitable conditions as have ever obtained, or are likely to obtain between two widely differing peoples inhabiting the same region. The records show a substantially unbroken up-surge of whites, and indicate an apparently inexorable depression and final engulfing of blacks.[2]

Universally, rural death rates are lower than death rates in urban districts, and this in spite of the fact that cities enjoy, to a considerable extent, self-selected populations.

---

[1] Thompson, W. S., *Population Problems*, N. Y., 1930, p. 191.

[2] It is unfortunate that these figures cannot be corrected to show the effect of migration, though that effect has been constantly exaggerated. See next chapter and Holmes, S. J., *Scientific Monthly*, vol. xxvii, pp. 557-561; also Dublin, L. I., *Health and Wealth*, pp. 270-271, New York, 1928.

PROPORTION OF WHITE AND COLORED PERSONS IN THE POPULATION
OF THE UNITED STATES

| | Percent | |
Census Year	White	Negro [1]
1790	80.7	19.3
1800	81.1	18.9
1810	81.0	19.0
1820	81.6	18.4
1830	81.9	18.1
1840	83.2	16.8
1850	84.3	15.7
1860	85.6	14.1
1870	87.1	12.7
1880	86.5	13.1
1890	87.5	11.9
1900	87.9	11.6
1910	88.9	10.7
1920	89.7	9.9

The more vigorous, imaginative, energetic and usually the
more healthy young men and women leave the farms and go
up to the city in search of greater economic, social, or political opportunities; remaining rural populations are of course
slightly sub-normal. The age advantage furthermore is in
favor of the cities: there are more very old people and infants in rural regions, and it is in these groups that death
rates are highest. Some students contend clamorously but
not entirely without reason, that cities may in the future
become quite as healthful or at least show quite as low death
rates as rural districts. The weight of opinion, however,
lies on the side of the view that, with economic status and
age composition equal, rural regions will always be more
healthful and show lower death rates than cities.[2]

Not only are infant death rates controlled largely by
wealth, but in general, life, death, health and disease are

[1] Percentage representing other colored strains has been deducted.

[2] Newsholme, *op. cit.*, pp. 275-276.

principally economic matters.[1]   The destruction of life among working people through accident and occupational disease of one or another sort is shocking.[2]   Far more significant, however, than the number of workers killed outright in industry is the large number of persons whose vitality is lowered and kept at a permanently sub-normal level by generally unhygienic conditions and especially by the fatigue of industrial or of household work.[3]   The death rate is everywhere lower among educated persons and among the rich than among the ignorant and the poor.[4]   The former live more protected and less exacting lives; they are better nourished; they command more adequate medical, surgical, dental, optical and psychiatric attention.[5]

The future course of the death rate will be in general downward, but there is an apparent lower limit.   Moreover, the vast saving recently made in infant mortality rates and in all death rates below the fortieth year may result later in a temporary upward swing in the general rate.   Statisticians in the Pennsylvania Bureau of Vital Statistics confirm in part this opinion.   By a process of extrapolation from current data they conclude that death rates will decline with constantly diminishing rapidity until a rate of 13.4 is reached in 1934.   From that point death rates will increase until in 1975 a rate of 15.0 is reached—due of course to the large number of deaths occurring among persons, who, subject to the circumstances of an earlier generation, would have died in infancy.[6]   Without some, at present, incredible

[1] Dublin, L. I., *Nineteenth Annual Meeting of the Tuberculosis Association*, 1923.

[2] Dublin, L. I., *Health and Wealth*, New York, 1928, p. 339.

[3] *Idem*, pp. 272-275.

[4] Newsholme, *op. cit.*, p. 497.

[5] Maciver, R. M., *Population Problems* (Dublin, L. I. ed'r), p. 289.

[6] *Vital Statistics Bulletin*, Pennsylvania Dept. of Health, Dec., 1929.

discovery in biology or in therapy it is quite probable that the ultimate limit of the general death rate is about 12.0.[1]

At this point it is perhaps not entirely impertinent to suggest that, whereas there is an apparent, and presumably inescapable, lower limit which the death rate may approach but never pass, *there is no real lower limit* to the birth rate— or rather, *it is zero*. Therefore, should the entire force of human intelligence and skill be brought to bear in reducing to their minima these two vital measures, it should be apparent even to a person of slightest mathematical proficiency that there is not the remotest danger of future over-population; and further, that with every passing moment, population pressure will constantly diminish.

In the decreasing death rate one finds only explanation of the growth of populations, a fact that needs no explaining— and further confirmation of the first clause of our formula: populations tend to increase as wealth increases. Throughout the present study, however, it has appeared that it is the slowness of population growth that presses hardest for explanation. That explanation must be reserved for a later chapter.

[1] Newsholme, *op. cit.*, p. 218.

CHAPTER XI

Migration

ALMOST universally, and quite mistakenly, immigration is deemed a local issue. Excepting the neglected point of view of population quality, and excepting comparatively sudden migrations, the ebb and flow and swirl of populations are locally insignificant. The migration of peoples, considered from the viewpoint of quality is of the deepest and broadest import; but the present work is concerned only with population growth. From the world point of view, migrations have no great effect upon the rate of human increase: a consequent mitigation of the conditions of existence makes room for some slight expansion in world population.

Birth and death, from the point of view of the individual, are mysteries. Even in this latest day, when purely accidental parenthood is losing its sanctity, the birth as well as the death of any individual seems entirely indeterminite. When however, groups of a hundred thousand or more are considered, birth rates and death rates become astoundingly definite. Persons interested in such matters predict without hesitation—or regret—that, for example, eighteen hundred out of each hundred thousand will die during the ensuing year and that twenty-three hundred will be born. Not only may birth rates and death rates be predicted by dead reckoning, extrapolation, but the underlying cause, the factor that governs all other causes of fluctuation in birth rates and death rates is becoming daily more apparent.

Differences in birth rates and death rates among several
regions and differences between those rates in the same
region for different times and classes are largely the result
of economic differences—though this may not be entirely
apparent in the case of birth rates until one remembers that
modern economic values are overwhelmingly psychological.[1]

Migrations are set in motion and kept moving principally
by economic considerations. In the United States there is a
well fostered tradition that a large proportion of American
emigrants left Europe mainly on account of political and
religious persecution and sought American soil that they
might live more fully and freely in the spiritual sense. It
is rather clear however, that in the beginning the Massachusetts Bay Company, for example, was a purely commercial enterprise—as was the earliest Virginia venture.[2]
The notably religious John Winthrop explains that he left
England because man, " the most precious of all creatures,
is here more vile and base than the earth we tread upon . . .
and thus it is come to pass, that children, servants, and
neighbors, especially if they be poor, are counted as the
greatest burdens, which if things were right would be the
chiefest earthly blessing." Winthrop goes on to say that
in addition, luxury in England had grown to such a height
of intemperance in all excess of riot, " as no man's estate
almost will suffice to keep sail with his equals." [3] Here is
rather a clear indication that possibly many of even the extremely religious early American immigrants were moved

[1] Schwiedland, E., *La population au point de vue economique, Rev.
d'Econ. Polit.*, Jan.-Feb., 1911, also see several references in chaps. xiv
and xvi.

[2] Channing, Edwin, *A History of the United States*, New York, 1905,
vol. i, p. 322.

[3] Winthrop, R. C., *Life and Letters of John Winthrop*, Boston, 1869,
vol. i, p. 309.

mainly by economic considerations. As early as 1846 European scholars held that the economic was the sole motive in emigrating to America.[1] If this is true of early immigrants, it should not require additional facts to convince the most intense American patriot that recent immigrants have been moved almost entirely by the desire to better their material welfare.[2]

Even comparatively momentary changes in welfare induce migration. Jerome says, " There is a close relation between the cyclical oscillations of employment and those of immigration and emigration " and there is " considerable reason to believe that this similarity . . . is due to a sensitiveness of migration to employment conditions." [3]

Intra-national migrations are, in their main currents, the swarming of young men and women to the cities and away from the farms. Such migrations have been going on forever, and professional alarmists in every generation have derived considerable profit from enlarging upon them. But so long as improvements in agriculture, in the storage of food and in the general technique of food production continue to multiply, less and less farm laborers will be required to support their fellows in the cities. Urbanization has unhealthy features, but far from being a " disease ", it has been forever the most ready measure of the progress of peoples and of nations.

All Americans are immigrants. This is true also of other peoples. The population of the world has been milling and swirling about forever. The existence of race is however conclusive evidence that most of this flowing and eddying

[1] van der Staten, Ponthoz, A., *Recherches sur la situation des émigrant aux États-Unis*, Brussels, 1846, pp. 19-20, 29-31.

[2] Abbott, E., *Historical Aspects of the Immigration Problem*, Chicago, 1926, pp. 23, 31, 38, 81, 210.

[3] Jerome, H., *Migration and Business Cycles*. New York, 1926. p. 243.

has been until a recent day almost entirely local. " It is interesting to note," says Haddon, " that despite all the movements which have taken place the distribution of the racial elements in the population of Europe is very similar to that of late Neolithic times." [1] Had the drift of world migrations been in the nature of trade winds instead of mild local drafts and eddies—in any but comparatively recent times— the mankind would not have remained long enough in any certain region to take on those deeply ingrained, locally common characteristics which, in sum, are called race. In recent years however, migrations have often become full and persistent currents—what Willcox calls the " proletarian mass migrations of the nineteenth and twentieth centuries." [2] Few persons today live in the houses occupied by their parents, and many families, by tracing their various residences through a dozen generations, would learn a great deal of geography. It is quite possible that as the mobility of populations increase, race will tend to disappear.

Granting that persons migrate to improve their economic position, it does not follow however, that if economic opportunities in Holland are greater than in Belgium, a large number of Belgians will instantly migrate to Holland; it does not necessarily follow that if living conditions in France are far better than in Spain, a large number of Spaniards will migrate to France; it does not follow that if one can make a better living in the United States than in Europe, a large portion of the population of Europe will migrate to America; but according to American opinion, the only barrier to such migration is the present quota law. Among nations and regions, variations in wealth have almost the same effect

[1] Haddon, A. C., *The Wanderings of Peoples*, Cambridge, England, 1912, p. 49.

[2] Willcox, W. F., *International Migrations*, New York, 1929, vol. i, p. 13.

upon population drift that variations in the level of water have upon its flow and distribution.[1] There is however this important difference; wherever *habitual* standards of living are low in the same proportion that poverty prevails, the tendency of population to flow from that region into a region of greater prosperity is offset or thwarted.[2]

It would be futile to argue that legal barriers, religious prejudice, national tradition and bonds of local attachment do not modify the general proposition that differences in economic opportunities set in motion streams of migration. For the purpose of a study in population growth it is only necessary however, to show that actual migrations are, almost without exceptions attempts to achieve easier living conditions or fuller material existence.

If the object of migrants is to find easier living conditions, the general effect of migration must be a softening of the struggle to cling to life, a net easing of population pressure. (The only alternative is to argue that migrants merely leap from frying pan to fire.)   This easing of population pressure by migration, though it is slight, offers—like the declining death rate—an explanation of population growth.

Though the general effect of migration is a slight mitigation of the life struggle, temporarily, population pressure becomes greater in the country that receives migrants, and there, birth rates decline.   The slight vacuum created in the country that loses population is soon filled by the product of a higher birth rate.   The net quantitative result, except for brief periods, is inconsiderable; over long reaches of time the effect is, for all practical considerations, *nil*.[3]

[1] Gregory, J. W., *Human Migration and the Future*, Philadelphia, 1927, p. 19.

[2] Fairchild, H. P., *Immigration*, New York, 1925, pp. 145-167.

[3] Walker, F. A., *Forum*, August, 1891; Fairchild, H. P., *The Paradox of Immigration*, American Journal of Sociology, 17: 254-257; East, E. M., *Report of World Population Conference*, London, 1927: East,

In a quantitative study of population it is not proper therefore to devote much attention to migration, but the net or actual effect of migrations is even today so hotly debated and so little understood that it can not be passed over without one or two more attempts at illumination: " The fact that certain English sparrows emigrated to America and there, by their remarkable fecundity and low standard of living displaced the native birds, has in no way affected the population of sparrows on English soil ". . . . " A similar thing is true with regard to the English people." [1]   These two perhaps hastily written sentences from Reuter bear in their principal meaning a very apt illustration of our main point.   Further on Mr. Reuter says, " With rare exceptions, the rate of growth of the United Kingdom seems not to have been disturbed by her remarkable emigration rate." [2]   England, for three centuries and more, has been pouring out her blood, her population, in every quarter of the globe.   Though this outpouring of vitality has not " disturbed " Great Britain's growth, there is little question that such a rapid loss of blood, extending over so many centuries, has resulted in depletion. Perhaps that will go far one day in explaining Great Britain's curious lack of power to recuperate from the effects of world war.

England, by an unexampled outpouring of sons—during three centuries—to develop the backward regions of the earth, may have lost a great many undesirable citizens; but in the main it was the more imaginative, the better equipped mentally and physically, the more dynamic from the ranks

E. M., *Heredity and Human Affairs*, New York, 1927, pp. 273-4; Mayo-Smith, *op. cit.*, pp. 21-26; Bushee, F. A., *Principles of Sociology*, New York, 1928, pp. 307, 316-24; for the opposed view see Gregory, *op. cit.*, pp. 19-21.

[1] *Op. cit.*, p. 185.

[2] *Scientific American*, 139: 340.

of her lower classes that she lost.[1] So long ago as the eighteenth century, Franklin pointed out that emigrants were in general a high-grade, self-selected people. In discussing Sadler's " law " of population, the *Edinburgh Review* for July, 1830 says, speaking of emigrants: " They are . . . a select class, even compared with that of their own age generally considered." [2] According to Sir George Knibbs: " Successful migration often demands that migrants shall be specially endowed as regards intelligence, courage and pertinacity. Not infrequently they must have a modicum of capital to succeed." [3] Moreover, society be it remembered, replenishes itself from the bottom; and if a nation loses constantly over a period of three hundred years the best of her lower classes, clearly, that nation is withering at the roots.

Let us attempt one more illustration of the slight effect of migration upon the quantitative aspect of human development. Between the sidewalk and the curb, in front of your house, there is a small plot of ground. Overflowing foot traffic and a summer drouth have made it almost bare; a tuft or two in favored regions comprise the entire grass population. To improve matters you throw a wire guard around the plot; you water it faithfully and add perhaps some grass food (fertilizer). Weeks pass: the original grass population has spread to the limits of the plot. Instead of looking to the offspring of the original scattered grass population to take up unoccupied regions, you might have sown strange seed—brought in the offspring of another plot, another land. In either case, the result is one: complete population of the well-fed, protected plot. The choice of foreign or domestic seed has in the end no quantitative bearing; though it will

[1] For opposite view see East, E. M., *Heredity and Human Afftirs*, New York, 1927, pp. 290-294.

[2] Vol. 51.

[3] *Scientific American*, 139: 340.

of course always effect the breed.[1]   Had all immigration to
the United States, for example, been cut off in 1850 the population would not differ greatly from its present number.
This ancient contention how has marshalled behind it hosts
of biologic and economic evidence.   If an amelioration in
living conditions warrants, population will increase and take
up the slack.   That this growth comes from immigration,
increased birthrate or decreased death-rate matters not; the
quantitative effect is in any case the same—and wholly the
result of more latitude in the conditions of existence.[2]

Migration is then from crowded regions of low living-
standards to regions where the standard of living is higher.
There seems to be a constant tendency to establish through
migrations a world-wide economic equilibrium—not however, a simple equilibrium like that resulting from the tendency of water to find one level, but an equilibrium of a
complex sort—an equilibrium between ratios obtained by
dividing wealth by the number of persons that must share
in it.   Migration, as pointed out on a preceding page, will
not always flow from a nation of low living-standards to one
of high living standards—at least the migration may be only
a matter of one or two especially dynamic and imaginative
individuals—for the great bulk of the people may be entirely
satisfied, on account of ignorance or inertia, with meager
living-standards.   Political, educational, climatic and other
conditions should also be taken into account.   Haddon says,
" Hunger and loot are not the only impulses toward migration." [3]   The desire to exchange the proprietorship of a
quiet Burgundian Vineyard for the ownership of a hot waffle
and scrapple stand in Middletown (U. S. A.) is not quite
universal.

[1] East and Jones, *Inbreeding and Outbreeding*, Philadelphia, 1919, chap.
vii, *passim*.

[2] *Cf.* Walker, F. A., *Forum*, August, 1891.

[3] Haddon, *op. cit.*, p. 3.

It is possible to lay too much emphasis upon the slight quantitative bearing of migrations; for biologists are generally agreed that, provided interbreeding is not carried on between too widely differing strains the mixed breed is stronger and more prolific than the pure. Migration promotes fecundity: strong additional support incidentally for the opinion (advanced in Chapter XIII) that human fecundit is not weaker in this modern day. As a matter of actual experience, all nations that have received large numbers of immigrants have discovered a higher birth rate among newcomers than among second, third, fourth or other generation residents of similar national origin.[1] Not only is there a markedly higher immigrant birth rate, but the birth rate among established residents diminishes more rapidly following a large wave of new immigration. This condition was noted and commented upon extensively by General Francis A. Walker, though as East very plainly shows, Walker did not originate the view but merely gave it vogue.[2]

Walker emphasized the effect of comparatively low living-standards in producing large families among American immigrants, and overlooked the revitalizing effect of outbreeding. A large proportion of American immigrants are unmarried and their subsequent marriages are—certainly more often than with native strains—distinctly exogamous. East and Jones have shown conclusively that exogamy result in marked increase in vigor and fecundity. It also appears that these qualities diminish rapidly in the second, third and fourth generations.[3] The decreasing size of families of first, second, third and fourth generation Americans is, as Walker maintained, the result of psycho-economic forces and

---

[1] *Cf*. East and Jones, *op. cit.*, pp. 161-162.

[2] Walker, F. A., *Forum*, August, 1891; East, *Heredity and Human Affairs*, New York, 1927, pp. 290-294.

[3] *Op. cit.*, chapter vii, *passim*.

therefore related to the hypothesis to which this book is devoted; but there is also some slight decrease in fecundity, an actual biologic change—if we may draw rather heavily upon the experience of plant and animal breeders—Walker in his alarm lest " native stocks " be supplanted appears to have overlooked three facts: (1) *all* American stocks are immigrant; (2) society replenishes itself from its lower layers and dies off at the top; (3) second and succeeding generation Americans take up indigenous living-standards with incredible alacrity.

Walker's principal thesis has been frequently misunderstood. His proposition is not that, had all immigration been halted in 1850, the population of the United States would be exactly what it is today; Walker's proposition is: assuming constant qualitative considerations in any population (especially wealth-producing abilities), numbers at any future date will be at most only temporarily affected by migration.[1] Or to return to the grass plot illustration: a certain area with a definite degree of fertility, given sufficient time, will become covered with grass regardless of whether all additions are from a small original tuft or whether there was an influx of foreign seed. The number of individual grass plants will reach the number warranted by conditions of space, fertility, moisture, and so on: beyond that number the grass population can not go, and below that number it will not fall. As in the general problem of population growth, fundamental factors determining migrations appear to be (1) the supply of material resources and human capabilities and (2) the height of living-standards.

Our net conclusion then must be that so far as the modern type is concerned, migration has the effect, locally and temporarily, of increasing or decreasing population; but taking

[1] Bushee, F. A., *Principles of Sociology*, New York, 1923, pp. 9, 309, 312-314.

into consideration long periods of time and the entire population of the world, the effect of migration upon population growth is negligible.   The migration of peoples from less to better favored regions does not of course differ in effect from the transportation of products of favored regions to areas where they are produced, if at all, only with great pains.   In fact the one may be properly called a migration of wants; the other, a migration of the means of satisfying wants.   In either case it is obvious that the aim is an amelioration of living conditions.   Migration makes way for population growth.   It offers an explanation, not of population constriction, but of expansion.   To find an explanation of the most significant fact in population growth, its slowness, one must turn to a study of birth rates.

CHAPTER XII

Birth Rates

In the opinion of Sir George Handley Knibbs, " It is a mysterious fact that, with the natural powers of human reproduction what they are, man numbers only 1950 millions, after the many eons that he has existed on earth." [1] The explanation of Sir George's enigma lay until recently, in extremely high death rates. Explanation of the modern sluggishness in population growth lies in dwindling birth rates.

Migration, it appears, relieves pressure here and fills a vacuum there, redistribution permits some slight expansion; but the final limitation of population size lies with the factors that govern death rates and birth rates. Birth rates however are fundamental; for they, of course, determine the amount of material upon which death rates operate.[2]

" The reproductive capacity of mankind, *fixed* [3] in the species through the selective processes of nature in a primitive or pre-human state of racial development, is sufficient to insure the perpetuation of the race under the most adverse

---

[1] *The Shadow of the World's Future*, London, 1928, p. 95.

[2] The term " birth rate " means the ratio between the number of living births in a year and the median number of persons alive during that year expressed in thousands; that is to say a birth rate of 14 means 14 births per thousand of the population. It is often called the " crude birth rate " to distinguish it from the refined or adjusted birth rate, which means the ratio of the number of live births to the number of married women of child-bearing age.

[3] Italics ours.

conditions it has had to meet." This sentence from Reuter is quoted not so much for its primary meaning—though its primary meaning is amply evidenced and extremely significant—it is because of the paramount importance of the word fixed.[1] The reproductive capacity of mankind in general is substantially fixed.

Of course it is not quite certain that the term fixed has any greater significance in this than in other connections. We speak of fixed stars, and we are not quite certain whether they are fixed or not. (In fact, astronomers describe their movements.) We speak of the number of teeth or the number of vertebrae in this or that mammal as being fixed; but they are not. Only in a qualified sense therefore may the term be used in discussing reproductive capacity. The reproductive capacity of the man kind is substantially fixed—though from millennium to millennium, and with radical changes in living conditions, it undoubtedly shows some slight variation. To speak however, of changes in birth rates, from generation to generation, as though they represented actual changes in fecundity or reproductive capacity shows extreme—carelessness. Fertility, fecundity, reproductive capacity have undergone very little change in the past generation, in the past hundred years, in the past thousand years; but birth rates have changed radically. This last however is not a matter of biology but of psychology— human cunning and intelligence.[2]

Many persons have assumed that a declining birth rate is tantamount to a shrinking population, and they have feared consequent disaster—either from thwarting the principal of

[1] Hexter, M. B., *Social Consequences of Business Cycles*, pp. 19 and 19 n.
[2] Crew, F. E. A., *Proceeding of the World Population Conf.*, 1927, p. 221; Dublin, L. I. (Ed'r) *Population Problems*, New York, 1926, p. 297; Sweeney, J. S., *The Natural Increase of Mankind*, Baltimore, 1926.

natural selection or from the wiping out of advanced peoples and cultures as a result of the differential nature of the declining birth rate; or they have feared that the present advanced economy or culture, which has resulted, in part, from the piling up of centers of population, would be lost, or at least diminished, if population did not continue to increase.

Many intelligent persons — even leading biologists, strangely enough—assume that a declining birth rate indicates a decline in propagating power or fecundity.[1] These credulous persons divide themselves into a number of schools. There are those who fear that urbanization brings a loss in fecundity, and there are those who believe that fecundity and education are adversely related. Others feel that the intelligent are less fecund than persons of smaller mental endowment. Doubleday advanced the idea that over-feeding lessens fertility. Sadler, thinking probably of urbanization, held that fecundity and population density are inversely proportioned. Professor Pearl, a century later, revives that opinion.[2] Delaney and even the great Darwin believed that culture and civilization repress human reproductive capacity. Spencer applied his theory of animal propagation rates to the human case and formulated the proposition that intellectual and spiritual development produce diminished fertility. Among leading modern authorities Nitti holds that inferior races are extremely fecund, while superior races have a naturally low reproductive capacity.[3]

Now the troublesome thing about these theories is that there is plausible evidence in support of any or all of them, just enough to suggest the color of truth, but not its sub-

[1] East, E. M., *Mankind at the Crossroads*, New York, 1923, p. 258.

[2] *Cf*. Pearl, R., *The Biology of Population Growth*, New York, 1925, p. 258.

[3] Newsholme, *op. cit.*, pp. 104-111; also *Proceedings of World Population Conference*, 1927, pp. 51, 56, 58, 219, 239, 241.

stance. It is quite true, for example, that the *birth rate* among educated persons is lower than among those who have had little or no formal training. Among college trained women the birth rate is incredibly low, but there is no evidence of correspondingly low fecundity.[1] The trouble here is precisely the one deplored in earlier chapters—a loose use of terms. Propagating power and fecundity are matters almost entirely apart from birth rates, they are determined in the course of millions of generations, a product of the rough and tumble of the struggle for existence—biologic matters. Birth rates on the contrary are governed by economic conditions and their psychological reflexes; they are the result of early or late marriage, of abstention from coition, of contraceptive devices, mechanical or chemical, for diverting the adventuresome little sperm in his determined course toward the ovum—or for destroying his tiny life.[2]

It is quite true that birth rates are lower in urban than in rural districts, lower among the " over-fed " than among the less abundantly nourished, lower among the cultured than among the uncultured; but differential birth rates are not in any way connected with culture, over-feeding, or city air and noises *per se;* current birth rates are almost entirely the " end products " of a purely psycho-economic process, and it happens that the factors in this process—economic competence, intelligence and education—are roughly correlated with civilization, urbanization and feeding. With the possible exception of feeding, they do not however, affect fecundity in any great degree.[3]

---

[1] First Report of *National Birth-Rate Commission*, E. P. Dutton, pp. 18, 20, 22, 25; also *Population Problems* (Dublin, L. I. Ed'r), pp. 34-36; also Baber & Ross, *Changes in the Size of American Families in One Generation*, pp. 61, 65, 67.

[2] Newsholme, *op. cit.*, pp. 106-108.

[3] *Idem.*

Let us examine the historical and statistical evidence.
Birth rates were not extremely high in pre-historic days.
Food was scanty, proper food for children was very difficult
to find, and food suitable for infants was wholly wanting.
From a study of modern primitives it may be inferred that
in prehistoric times a long period of lactation was required;
children were suckled for three, five or possibly eight years,
which meant of course wide spacing of births, perhaps not
more than four or five during the entire child-bearing
period.[1]   The child-bearing period was shorter than in
modern times, and life too on the average was shorter.
Perilous and difficult living conditions made an extremely
high birth rate impossible.[2]

It is quite probable that birth rates may have had some
slight age-long decline.   There is, however the strong possibility of a perceptible upward trend during the Middle Ages.
By the end of the seventeenth century the trend was distinctly downward.   Crum found that for certain classes of
American wives the average number of children decreased
between the years 1700 and 1880 from 7.37 to 2.77.[3]   But
it was not until the last quarter of the nineteenth century that
the declining birth rate changed rapidly enough to attract
universal attention.[4]   Education, improved means of communication and better transportation facilities brought into
remotest parts knowledge of better levels of living, and often
the desire to enjoy higher living-standards.   As a result
various contraceptive practices began to accentuate sharply

[1] Carr-Saunders, A. M., *The Population Problem*, Oxford, 1922, pp.
137, 165, 174, 196, 225.

[2] East, *op. cit.*, pp. 329-30.

[3] Crum, F. S., " The Decadence of Native American Stock," *Qu. Pub.
Am. Stat. Assn.*, September, 1914.

[4] Kuczynski, R. R., *The Balance of Births and Deaths*, New York,
1928, p. 5.

the declining birth rate.[1]   In fact it is probable that the fall in birth rates has been underestimated, for improved channels of information have made possible the reporting of a constantly larger proportion of births.[2]

Although falling birth rates are universal, the recent, accentuated decline did not begin at the same time in all countries.[3]   In America it began early in the present century; in France, during the decade following 1860; in England and Wales the first sharp drop took place after 1880; and in Germany, not until toward the end of the nineteenth century.[4]

Some idea of the rapidity with which contraceptive practices spread during the latter half of the nineteenth century and the early years of the twentieth century is suggested by the fall in French birth rate between 1885 and 1909.   The decline was from 24.7 to 19.6, a matter of 20.6 per cent.[5]

In England, from the fifties to the eighties of the past century, the birth rate was approximately constant.[6]   For the period 1881-1885, it was 33.5; in 1909 it was 25.8—a decline of 23.0 per cent.   (There was no corresponding drop in the marriage rate.)[7]   By 1913, the English birth rate had fallen to 24.1.   For 1918, the last war year, it was 17.7;[8]   immediately after the close of the war there was a temporary increase, but during 1928 the birth rate declined

[1] Dublin, L. I., *Health and Wealth*, New York, 1928, Diagram, p. 198.

[2] Chaddock, R. E., *Principles and Methods of Statistics*, New York, 1925, p. 30.

[3] Hexter, M. B., *Social Consequences of Business Cycles*, New York, 1925, p. 105.

[4] Kuczynski, R. R., *The Balance of Births and Deaths*, New York, 1928, p. 11.

[5] Hexter, M. B., *op. cit.*, Table, p. 15.

[6] Yule, G. U., *The Fall of the Birth Rate*, Cambridge, 1920, p. 8.

[7] Yule, G. U., *op. cit.*, p. 11.

[8] *Second Report of the National Birth-Rate Commission*, London, 1918-1920, p. xxxl.

to 15.7. Again, there was no corresponding drop in the marriage rate.[1]

In nations ordinarily considered backward members of the Western Civilization, the decline in birth rates was less marked during the period 1885-1909: In Italy the decline was 14.7 per cent, in Spain, 14.4 per cent, in Ireland, 1.6 per cent. In those productive and progressive British dominions, where standards of living, intelligence and education are high, the decline in birth rates was greater: New Zealand, 25.5 per cent; New South Wales, 28.4 per cent; South Australia, 25.8 per cent. The lowest birth rates are nearly always found in the highly civilized, urbanized parts of the earth; France, England, Belgium—with an average birth rate of perhaps 18.5.[2] The highest birth rates in the Western Civilization appear in agricultural, semi-barbaric regions: Bulgaria, Rumania, Russia, with an average birth rate of perhaps 39.5—more than twice as great as in regions where standards of living are higher.

Though vital statistics in the United States are unsatisfactory, it is probably fair to say that throughout the nation the average birth rate in 1929 was about 21.5;[3] the actual rate for registration areas in 1927 was 20.6.[4] The trend of the birth rate may be unmistakeably inferred however from census figures which show the number of children less than five years old for each thousand women of child-bearing age. In 1860 the number was 634; in 1890 it was 485; in 1920, only 422. The average size of the American family shows

---

[1] Report of the Registrar-General for England and Wales (No. 320), London, 1929.

[2] Kuczynski, op. cit., p. 7.

[3] Cf. Newsholme, op. cit., pp. 72-74.

[4] U. S. Dept. of Commerce, Births, etc.,: 1927, part II, Washington, 1929, p. 7.

a similar trend: in 1860 it was 5.3; in 1890, 4.9; in 1920, only 4.3.[1]

A lower marriage rate and a higher age at marriage have often been advanced in explanation of lower birth rates, but Thompson and several other students have found these influences—if they exist at all—to be generally overestimated.[2] Duncan finds moreover that the fertility, and probably the fecundity, of women increases with age up to about the thirtieth year—when the probability of producing twins reaches its greatest height.   There is no record of triplets occurring before the mother's twenty-sixth year or earlier than the second pregnancy.[3]   The fall in the birth rate is not in any significant sense the result of a lower marriage rate or a higher age at marriage;[4] it is due it will appear from the data submitted below, to a definitely planned smaller number of children per family.[4]

Modern birth rates are almost wholly determined by psychologic and economic forces; they are governed almost entirely by the strength of the desire for higher living-standards.   Birth rates and the desire for higher standards of living are inversely correlative; a strong desire for higher living-standards results in a lower birth rate.   But birth rates are also directly related to general prosperity: even comparatively minor increases as well as the more conspicuous improvements in general welfare are reflected in a larger

[1] Bossard, J. H. S., *Problems of Social Well-Being*, New York, 1927, p. 116 (based on the work of Wilcox).

[2] Thompson, W. R., *Population Problems*, New York, 1930; First Report of *National Birth-Rate Commission*, E. P. Dutton & Co.

[3] Duncan, J. M., *Fecundity, Fertility and Sterility*, Edinburgh, 1871, pp. 70-75.

[4] Baber & Ross, *op. cit.*, pp. 45-46, 48-51; also Dublin, L. I., *Health and Wealth*, New York, 1928, p. 180.

number of births; depressed or uncertain economic conditions reduce the number of births.[1]

The effect of economic uncertainty upon the birth rate became very distinct during the World War [2] — though the changes in birth rates noted below cannot be entirely accounted for of course by varying degrees of "economic uncertainty." In England and Wales the net loss of population resulting from low war-time birth rates is estimated at 500,000. The actual birth rate fell from 23.8, in 1914, to 17.7 in 1918—in spite of a remarkable increase in the number of marriages during early war years.[3] The Registrar-General's estimate is that 200,000 persons were married during the period 1914 to 1917 who in the ordinary course of events would have remained single. With the return of peace and greater economic security the birth rate bounded exuberantly up to 25.5 in 1920; but with the coming of post-war business depression, culminating in 1924, births dwindled: the rate became 18.2. Later came the Dawes Plan and a new hope of prosperity for Europe; this new hope was reflected in a sightly higher birth rate in 1925; 18.3. (During a period of almost universally sagging rates, an upturn of 0.1 is of course far more significant than a drop five times as great.) The Dawes Plan advanced definitely the prosperity of nearly every country in Europe; only in Great Britain did business, after a slight revival, relapse to dismal levels; the English birth rate dropped, in 1928, to 15.7.[4] The French birth rate was low before the

[1] First Report *National Birth-Rate Commission* (Great Britain), pp. 290-291; also Kuczynski, *op. cit.*, pp. 6-7; also *World Population Conference*, 1927, pp. 209-210; also Dublin, L. I., *Problems of Population*, New York, 1926, p. 289.

[2] Second Report of the *National Birth-Rate Commission*, London, 1918-1920, pp. 39-44.

[3] *Report*, Registrar-General, England and Wales, 1928.

[4] *Report*, Registrar-General, England and Wales, 1929.

war—in 1913 it was 19.0 and in 1914 it was 18.0—but during the last year of the war it fell to 10.4. Everywhere, the rapidity of war-time decline in the number of births was sharply accentuated. Among advanced peoples, such is the effect of economic uncertainty upon the birth rate.[1]

The extraordinary fall in birth rates in France, Prussia, Bavaria, England and Wales during the World War was, according to Professor Pearl, due in part to hard living conditions, but he adds, " Here, however, the psychological also had a large role." [2]   In either case, it seems that economic conditions controlled—controlled directly, through " hard living conditions ", and according to the second statement, indirectly, through fear of lowered living-standards, or rather, through the desire to retain high living-standards. These conclusions accord perfectly with that we have called, in developing our formula, the psycho-economic control of population growth.

Further evidence that the control of birth rates is mainly economic, or rather psycho-economic, is presented by the behavior of 1915 to 1927 birth rates in the United States, where the war danger was of course remote. Rates fell steadily, as the increasing uncertainty of the war brought constantly greater economic uncertainty. In 1919 there was an especially sharp drop in the number of births. As a matter of fact the war ended a year earlier, 1918, but the period of gestation must be taken into account. With the coming of post-war prosperity and the assurance that returning soldiers and post-war immigration would not imperil jobs, birth rates actually ran *upward* during 1920 and

---

[1] Second Report of *National Birth-Rate Commission, loc. cit.*; Bunle, R., *Relation entre les variations des indices economiques et le mouvement des mariages*, Journ. Soc. Stat., March, 1911; Schwiedland, E., *La population au point de vue Economique*, Rev. d'Econ. Pol., Jan.-Feb., 1911.

[2] Pearl, Raymond, *Science* (N. S.), vol. 51.

1921. Since that time there has returned the steady universal downward trend which results from striving for ever higher living-standards.[1] Moreover, Doctor Thomas found that for a long series of *pre-war* years in England and Wales both marriage and birth rates followed very closely the ebb and flow of business conditions.[2]

Children are a burden; they are an expense; they destroy freedom and smother the ego. The ego must feed and grow or perish; it waxes and fattens best on freedom—freedom in its widest meaning. Nothing is so devastating to freedom, even among the rich, as children. Though a man and woman never see their children still they must refrain from doing and must deny themselves much they might do or have were it not for the presence of these perverse extensions of personality.

What possible justification can an educated person in this second quarter of the twentieth century find in propagation? An extension of ego? A contrary process however by which the ego, in attempting to extend self beyond self, destroys self. Throughout animal and plant life there are countless examples of an almost immediate destruction of the female parent in this perverted exercise of self esteem. In modern society, where a vast, complicated system of economy throws nearly the whole cost, and the entire burden of final responsibility, in *rearing* off-spring upon the male, who by eons of totally different experience has been made wholly unfit emotionally for this responsibility, the male and his ego often find an untimely end.

The most rational justification for propagation is that, when properly proportioned to economic competency it is a

[1] U. S. Dept. of Commerce *Births, etc. 1927*, Washington, 1929, p. 7.

[2] Thomas, D. S., *Social Aspects of the Business Cycle*, New York, 1927, p. 155.

means of extending self and of gaining an emblematic or representative immortality—in foreshortened human sense. Or possibly, children may be considered in a category with riding-horses, rare antiques and acquired talents, sources of amusements, means of developing self-esteem, of developing the sense of power and well-being, which often results in an actual strengthening of the ephemeral precious physical self. Having children for the greater glory of God or Country, which is to say the manufacture of pew renters and cannon fodder, is not in the modern mode.

The age-long propaganda of priest and military chief has nevertheless confirmed the overwhelming majority of mankind in the opinion that there is inherent virtue in having children, that it is not only a moral process but that it is morality, and that the thwarting of any detail of the process (except enjoyment) is itself the essence of immorality. Children are in some unexplained way more than self-appendages upon which the ego may possibly feed — frequently however with disastrous results.[1] As long ago as 1896, A. T. Hadley, careful and conservative scholar, said:

It is true that as society exists at present, high comfort and low birth rate are commonly associated, because comfort is made to depend upon prudence. Let the comfort be made independent of prudence, as in the case of the pauper or criminal and the birth rate tends to increase rather than diminish. *It may not be exactly true, as some Malthusians would have us believe, that the low birth rate is the cause of the comfort, but it is much farther from the truth to assert that the comfort is the cause of the low birth rate. Both are the result of a common cause— the exercise of prudence, which gives high comfort and low birth rate to those who are capable of practising it, while those who are incapable of so doing have at once a higher birth rate and a lower level of comfort.[2]*

[1] *Idem*, p. lxxiii; also First Report *National Birth-Rate Commission*, London, 1918-1920, pp. 1-5, 282-284, 389-390.

[2] Hadley, A. T., *Economics*, New York, 1896, p. 48.   Italics ours.

Here of course we have another statement, this time by an extremely reliable authority, of the second clause of our hypothesis.

The immediate cause of the declining birth rate is simple and obvious: conscious restriction of births. " There are no grounds for suspecting that any other factor is at work": strong language from so careful a scholar as Carr-Saunders.[1] Evidence has piled up to prodigious heights, but no reasonable person would seek beyond the fact that average fecundity among modern, civilized women amounts to a total production of ten to twelve children,[3] while the *actual* average number of children in families of western civilization is less than three.

Furthermore, no thoughtful person will enter into tedious statistical examinations of this or that hypothesis of changing fecundity or fertility which might or might not explain a variation of a hair's breadth one way or another, when the fact that wants explaining is the difference between an actual family of less than three and a potential family of more than ten. Or in East's phrasology, the potential fecundity of the human race should be represented by a birth rate of about 60.0, while actual birth rates in the Western Civilization average about 20.0.[4] The birth rate is a purposefully controlled phenomenon rising and falling in response to the plans and prejudices of individuals influenced mainly by economic considerations. To seek explanation of declining birth rates in a mysterious and universal pathological change is a perversion of effort.

Birth control is the valve that controls variations in the

[1] Carr-Saunders & Jones, *Social Structure of England and Wales*, London, 1927, p. 222.

[2] Wattal, P. K., *The Population Problem in India*, Bombay, 1916, p. 7; Duncan, J. M., *Fecundity, Fertility and Sterility*, Edinburgh, 1871, p. 112; Carr-Stunders, *op. cit.*, pp. 99, 100.

[3] East, E. M., *Mankind at the Crossroads*, New York, 1923, p. 347.

flow of human life; it is the influence that determines modern birth rates and the size of modern families.[1] It gives promise of being universally considered by the next generation to be as obviously desirable as voluntary church membership or voluntary marriage.

The new freedom of women has affected birth rates. Until comparatively recent years, the only honorable way for a woman to earn a living was to submit to being used as a child-bearing machine. " Civilization can not be kept alive and transmitted undiminished to posterity, if the members of the educated classes think it is a burden to have large families, and if even the women prefer to find some other vocation in life than that of bearing children and educating them." [2] A thousand other occupations have since come into competition with this single, age-long employment. Not three generations ago, women who dared deny that their whole meaning in the world was the production of babies were so few as to be curiosities. Today a large percentage of the women of the world have found interesting and lucrative employments that have nothing to do with the production of children. In fact among women today the curiosity, the infrequent case, is the woman who insists that she is principally a child-bearing machine, and that womankind can have no other important meaning. This complete reversal of the common conception of the primary meaning of women has cut sharply into birth rates.[1]

The nineteenth-and-twentieth-century shrinkage in average family size has progressed rapidly, especially in late years, and there is every possibility that birth rates will con-

[1] *World Population Conference*, 1927, pp. 153-154; also Dublin, *op. cit.,* p. 39.

[2] Bowen, Francis, " Malthusianism, Darwinism and Pessimism," *North American Review*, 1879, p. 472.

[3] Dublin, L. I., *Problems of Population*, New York, 1926, pp. 235, 237, 238, 240, 241; *World Population Conference*, London, 1927, p. 210.

tinue to decline. For it is the most numerous classes and the most numerous races of the earth that lack the information necessary for the triumph of ego over sex—in their merciless, immemorial, hand-to-hand struggle. Ego, especially among the lower classes of mankind, has been forever the slave of sex. At the moment that is passing there appears a growing probability that the relationship can be reversed. An organized effort to deprive, particularly the less successful classes, of information necessary to the fuller expression of self cannot be forever successful. In spite of religious and military opposition, that information will reach backward races and depressed classes.

It is doubtful if the church will ever desert entirely its present position, for thereby it would expose to destruction some of the heaviest trunk-lines of theologic dogma, but it is quite possible that an enlightened—or repressed—military party will soon find that a high grade, fully expressed population is far better able to take care of itself than a merely numerous, low-grade people. Strong and almost wholly unresented gestures toward informing the numerous classes concerning the technique of contraception have been made by such slow-moving official organizations as the Japanese, British and Dutch governments. As information spreads to the poorer classes the fall in the birth rate should become far more marked, because the poor is not only the largest class, but a class of notorious propagators. Should ground appear for belief that the birth rate was falling too rapidly it is probable that it could be arrested at any point—or almost indefinitely raised—by the simple expedient of governmental provision for offspring, which would permit the ego of individuals the stimulus derived from completing the parental process and at the same time relieve the great unsuited majority of the burden of parental responsibility and attendant loss of freedom.

CHAPTER XIII

The Dysgenic Trend

BIRTH RATES are declining everywhere, but at paces that differ among economic, intellectual, educational and social classes — and among races, nations and religions. When birth rates are higher at one end of a classification than at the other, there is said to be a differential birth rate within the group. When birth rates within a general group are lower among classes possessing a superior natural inheritance the differential birth rate is said to show a dysgenic trend—though of course there is not necessarily depreciation in quality so long as there is a compensatory differential death rate.[1]

According to Newsholme, the differential birth rate is an ancient characteristic of the human race.[2] Its chief bearing is upon the quality of population. Quantity must in the long run, however, be affected by quality. Upon the character of the differential birth rate depends the outcome of such fundamental questions as, Who shall persist and prevail throughout the world: the white race or some other, the physically fit or the physically unfit, the intellectually capable or the comparatively unintellectual?[3]

---

[1] There is of course broad ground for criticizing this material concerning dysgenic trends, on the ground that it weakens our formula. Here however we are not attempting to defend a theory or an alleged law, we are endeavoring to illuminate and determine the probable field of application and the probable degree of accuracy of an hypothesis.

[2] Newsholme and Stevenson, *Jour. Royal Stat. Society*, vol. 59.

[3] Sweeney, J. S., *The Natural Increase of Mankind*, Baltimore, 1926, pp. 35-36; *World Population Conference*, London, 1927, p. 154.

There is surprisingly little agreement among experts as to the facts, let alone the interpretation of differential birth rates. One finds authority for the opinion that the general level of quality is rising, and as good authority for the opposite opinion. One can even find authority for the opinion that the differential birth rate between certain regions works this way or that: there are those who believe that the birth rate is declining more rapidly in Europe than in America and there are those who believe the contrary.[1] Some students find that the birth rate in rural regions is declining more rapidly than the birth rate in urban regions, and there are those who maintain an opposite view. Able scholars and engaging writers conclude that the white race is being gradually engulfed and destroyed by other races; and there are possibly even more earnest scholars, if not quite such engaging writers, who maintain that the white race will prevail.

That the birth rate is very closely related to social and economic status appears to be an established fact. As long ago as 1911, Emerick concluded that the diminishing birth rate is primarily volitional, the end-product of a psychological process, governed by economic circumstances.[2] The rate is lowest among the highest cultural and economic classes, and highest among the lowest classes.[3]

On the lower east side of New York City the birth rate in 1927 was four times as high as on Park Avenue—that is to say, in one neighborhood, a birth rate four times as high as in another, removed from it but a few city blocks.[4]

[1] *World Population Conference*, London, 1927, p. 158.

[2] Emerick, G. F., "Is the Diminishing Birth-Rate Volitional?", *Pop. Sci. Mo.*, 78: 80.

[3] Dublin, L. I., *Problems of Population*, New York, 1926, p. 289; *World Population Conference*, London, 1927, pp. 131, 132, 134, 140, 144, 161, 162, 195, 203-207, 221, 222, 244.

[4] Report, *Bellevue-Yorkville Health Demonstration*, New York, 1928.

ANNUAL BIRTHS PER 1,000 WOMEN OF FERTILE AGE IN DIFFERENT
ECONOMIC STRATA [1]

Classification	Paris	Berlin	Vienna	London
Very poor quarters	108	157	200	147
Poor quarters	95	129	164	140
Comfortable quarters	72	114	155	107
Very comfortable quarters	65	96	153	107
Rich quarters	53	63	107	87
Very rich quarters	54	47	81	63
Average	80	102	153	109

Pearson, using the data of Rubin and Westergaard, found
the average size of families to be 4.52 for professional
classes, 4.58 for commercial classes, and 4.95 for artists.
More interesting, however, he found the *survival* rate as between professional and commercial classes reversed.   The
number of children per family who reached reproductive age
was 3.31 for professional classes, 3.01 for commercial
classes, and 3.14 for artists.   Possibly the children of professional people are more intelligently reared.[2]

From the face value of the evidence one must conclude
that there is a dysgenic trend in birth rates.   Recent figures
on the relative prolificness of married men of various occupations in England and Wales in terms of the number of
offspring per hundred married couples follow: for teachers
95, Non-Conformist ministers 96, Church of England clergy
101, physicians and surgeons 103, authors and editors 104,
policemen 153, postmen 159, carmen 207, dock laborers 231,
barmen 234, miners 258, and general laborers 438.[3]   One
must not draw too fine lines; for example, it is perfectly
clear that the occupation of policeman demands a wide

[1] Reuter, E. B., *Population Problems, Philadelphia*, 1923, p. 241.

[2] *Cf. World Population Conference*, London, 1927, p. 37; Kuczynski,
R. R., *The Balance of Births and Deaths*, New York, 1922, p. 54.

[3] Pearl, R., *Problems of Overpopulation* (M. Sanger, Ed'r), New
York, 1926, p. 18.

range of abilities, but there seems to be nevertheless a distinct qualitative difference between persons suitable for this occupation and occupations preceding it in the classification just given. There seems also to be room for the inference that there is a wide qualitative difference between " miners 258 " and a " general laborers 438." At any rate it is a far cry from the type that produces 95 children to that which has an output of 438 children per hundred married couples.[1]

There are those who maintain that the inverse relationship between family size and economic competence is not fundamentally significant, because economic competence is not a measure of native ability or worth. Although economists agree that economic competence is not a precise measure of social worth—and that in some cases these two seem utterly dissociated or even inversely related—if it were not true that inherent skill or capacity in production and consequent economic competence is a good rough measure of social worth, the age-old and at present dominant type of competitive civilization would long since have ceased developing; for the promise of economic competency has always been its mainspring of constructive effort.[2]

Numerous studies show that the marriage rate for highly educated persons is lower than for the general population, and that age at marriage is greater. Moreover, the number of children per marriage is smaller.[3] In the United States, this is true alike of men and women graduates of co-educational institutions and other colleges and universities.[4]

Less than half of all college women marry before the age

[1] *World Population Conference*, London, 1927, pp. 192-193; Newsholme, Sir A., *op. cit.*, pp. 108-109.

[2] Cf. *World Population Conference*, 1927, London, p. 149.

[3] First Report of *National Birth-Rate Commission*, London, 1918-1920, pp. 18-20.

[4] Dublin, L. I., *Health and Wealth*, New York, 1928, pp. 239-242.

of forty, which is far less than the general rate for the state of Massachusetts with eighty per cent, or for the United States with ninety per cent—or the state of Arkansas, with ninety-six per cent. The average age at marriage for college women (26.4) is greater by about two years than the age at marriage for women in their immediate families and among their friends who are not college graduates. A study made in 1900 showed the average age for sisters of college women to be 24.2, for their cousins 24.7 and for their friends 24.2; it was also found that the better grade of students married later. Phi Beta Kappas show a marriage rate which is slightly less than for college women in general.

College men show a similar inclination to delay or avoid marriage and to restrict the size of families, but not quite to the extent shown by college women.[1] The average number of children among married graduates of Harvard and Yale fell from about 3.25 for the decade ending 1860 to little more than 2.00 for the decade ending 1890;[2] and Dublin has demonstrated that even with the reduced modern death rate a family-size of 3.17 is necessary for self-perpetuation.[3] It is clear that college men and women are not reproducing their own numbers.

There appears to be a differential between birth rates in native and immigrant American families. The Immigration Commission's recent investigation showed the average number of children for native white women of native parentage, married from ten to twenty years, to be 2.7 children; while the average number for white women of foreign parentage was 4.4. Foreign-born women who bore no children amounted to 5.7 per cent; women of native parentage having

[1] *World Population Conference*, 1927, London, pp. 151-152.

[2] Baber and Ross, *op. cit.*, pp. 59-62.

[3] On account of the declining death rate Dublin reduced this figure later to 3.15 (see Dublin, L. I., *Health and Wealth*, New York, 1928, p. 204.

no children amounted to 13.0 per cent. Forty per cent of the women of native parentage had one to two children. Only nineteen per cent of the foreign-born women had so few as one or two children. Only ten per cent of native women of native parentage had five or more children.[1]

In 1890 the number of children under five years of age per thousand native white mothers in the United States was 777 and for foreign-born mothers 1,159. In 1910 the number of children for each thousand native mothers had fallen to 706; for foreign-born mothers, 1,119. Nevertheless the 1910 *ratio* of native- to foreign-mother births, .639, was *more favorable to native white mothers* than the 1890 ratio of .617. But the question as to whether or not the earlier American stock shall persist remains in dispute. Statistics adequate to a settlement of the question are not available. A slight balance of present evidence seems to favor the offspring of recent arrivals, but the *trend* of the differential rate (as shown here and in later paragraphs) suggests the final prevalence of the earlier white American stock.[2]

The negro birth rate in the United States has declined rapidly. In fact, it is at present lower than the birth rate for foreign-born whites.

Although there may remain some slight room to doubt that the balance of life forces has turned definitely in favor of the white race, it appears from the table below that the ratios of differentials are shifting rapidly. The *trend* favors the whites.

Furthermore it appears that, while the colored birth rate was 29.1 per cent greater than the white birth rate in the United States in 1926, the colored death rate was 63.2 per

[1] U. S. Dept. of Labor, *Children's Bureau*, B. P., 119, pp. 46-48; Dublin, L. I., *Health and Wealth*, New York, 1928, p. 179.

[2] Thompson, W. S. (chapter in *Population Problems*, Dublin, L. I., Ed'r, New York, 1926, p. 39; also Baber and Ross, *op. cit.*, p. 29.

NUMBER OF CHILDREN UNDER FIVE YEARS OF AGE PER 1,000 WOMEN OF
CHILD BEARING AGE (15-44 YEARS) [1]

	Negro	White	Ratio
1880	760	586	1.29
1890	621	517	1.20
1900	582	508	1.14
1910	519	484	1.07
1920	431	471	.91

cent greater than white.[2]   When the marked death-rate differential in favor of the white population is taken into account, it becomes obvious that in the struggle for final prevalence between white and colored races, the white race will prevail.[3]

Another differential appears in current birth rates: there are relatively fewer births in urban than in rural regions. Furthermore, differences in birth rates between city and country are greater for colored populations than for whites.[4] As whites become urbanized, birth rates fall; but as colored peoples urbanize, birth rates fall more rapidly.   Here is further evidence to support our hypothesis that, as colored races enter and take part in the Western civilization, their absorption and final extinction will progress more rapidly.   Adding this evidence to the differential death rate in favor of the white race and the favorable differential *trend* of adverse differential birth rates, there remains little room for doubt that this hypothesis will soon be completely established.

The existing differential between urban and rural birth

[1] U. S. Dept. of Commerce, *Bureau of Census*, Negro Population in the United States, 1790-1915," 1918; U. S. *Census of 1920*, vol. ii.

[2] U. S. Dept. of Commerce, *Births, etc.*, 1926, pt. i, p. 7.

[3] East is very positive on this point. See *Mankind at the Crossroads*, New York, 1923, pp. 12-15. For divergent view see Holmes, S. H., *Scientific Monthly*, vol. 27, pp. 557-561.

[4] Reuter, E. B., *Population Problems*, Philadelphia, 1923, p. 247 (better census bulletin).

rates is a world-wide phenomenon.[1] In earliest times birth rates began declining in the cities, but in recent decades the rural decline has been more rapid. It is possible that this differential may disappear. In fact, 1926 statistics for the United States show an urban birth rate of 21.2 and a rural rate of only 20.1.[2] With improved means of transportation, communication and education carrying information outward from centers of civilization to rural and outlying districts, intelligent residents in these regions have been learning the means of keeping family size within bounds.

Now the question arises, what changes in the rate of growth and quality of populations will result from the differentials existing between white and colored races, between urban and rural regions, between crude and cultured stocks? If the more prolific are at the same time the less capable, and if their lack of capacity is in any large sense hereditary, the quality of populations must be constantly declining— assuming, of course, that there is not a compensating differential death rate, but beyond a doubt, there is at least in part. If this opposed differential in death rates more than offsets the differential in birth rates, the resulting, reversed differential will insure a constantly improving population.

Then there is the indisputable and comprehensive fact which biologists call *variation*—including *accidents, mutants* or *sports*—which means that in the perpetuation of those two grand human strata called the upper and lower classes of society, there are, in the upper class, a great many downward variants and in the lower class a great many upward variants. There are furthermore two commonly accepted facts which lead unmistakably to the conclusion that the resultant of upward and downward variants is upward. First, there is the fact that every great person, however superbly

[1] *World Population Conference*, 1927, London, p. 149.
[2] U. S. Dept. of Commerce, *Births, etc.*, 1926, Washington, 1928, p. 7.

made and mannered, was not very long ago a clodhopper, or his grandfather was — or some not very remote ancestor. There is not a philosopher, a king, a scientist, merchant prince, toe dancer or statesman who need dig back many generations to fetch up the aroma of sod. Again, we have the fact that there is no poised state in the bio-universe; every existing species is progressing or decaying. The mere presence of a species is complete testimony to the fact that until very recently, for thousands of generations at any rate, that species has been progressing. (The word progress, of course, is assumed to have no meaning beyond adaptation to the conditions of existence, and, without stepping clear of the world of reality this is possibly the only water-tight definition of progress that can be made.) [1]

Plainly, the human kind, considered as made up of a number of strata representing different degrees of superiority and inferiority, replenishes itself from the bottom and dies off at the top. (It is an interesting hypothesis that this dying off at the top may be the result of the greater emotional strain due to a fuller—more frantic—way of living.[2]) The point in discussion is perhaps illuminated by the data evidencing differential birth rates between urban and rural regions. There are many accepted facts which go to prove that in general it is the more capable young men and women who move up to the city from rural regions in search of better opportunities for the exercise of their talents, indicating it would seem an extremely dysgenic process: an over-prolific, low-grade, rural population constantly replen-

[1] This point was developed at some length by the present author in a brief article, *Progress—By Accident or Plan*, Scientific Monthly, February, 1925; also cf. *World Population Conference*, London, 1927, pp. 167, 202, 342; *Population Problems* (Dublin, Ed'r), New York, 1926, p. 5; Dublin, L. I., *Health and Wealth*, New York, 1928, pp. 226-228.

[2] Compare Pell, C. E., *The Law of Births and Deaths*, London, 1921, pp. 37-43.

ishing a high-grade, low-birth-rate city stock. The saving feature here is again the biologic fact of variants or sports: that is to say, a considerable number in each generation differ markedly from their parents in ways that make them distinctly superior; and it is mainly such persons who move up from the country and replenish urban populations. Furthermore, of the remaining, run-of-the-bin and worse individuals who in general remain in rural regions, large numbers do not survive to perpetuate their kind. Such a broad hypothesis or generalization can of course be offset by equally apparent though perhaps not quite so significant propositions — as, for example, the fact that among those who migrate to cities there is always an over-emotional, undercapable group, those who carry more sail than ballast, and who often become criminals or social debtors of one sort or another; then there are of course many otherwise superior persons who remain in country districts because of low emotionality or lack of imagination.

Interest in inferiority centers naturally upon the possibility of eliminating inferior individuals, or rather of reducing their number, mainly by preventing them from reproducing their kind—though in some few instances inferiority in an individual is curable. To attempt the elimination or reduction of inferior classes is very generally accepted as legally and morally sound; it remains only to define—and to devise methods of detecting—precisely what constitutes inferiority, and to determine the best means of eliminating or reducing it.

The elimination or reduction of inferiority is accomplished in part by natural means. It is well known that the birth rate among the insane is generally low; among epileptic as well as among extremely feeble-minded persons it is almost zero. Furthermore, so far as the demonstrably inferior are concerned, the death rate is far higher than among normal persons. Defectives of all sorts are notoriously shortlived.

The general opinion that inferior classes are increasing rapidly must also be amended by the consideration that, as a result of improved technique among experimental psychologists, large numbers of persons are being recognized as inferior, who in earlier generations would not have been detected. The increasing complexity and rapidly changing conditions of modern life are furthermore forcing constantly larger numbers of the weaker members of society into various dependent groups; this also creates an impression of widening inferiority. The more humane and intelligent care recently given to such groups lengthens their life-span considerably, adding thereby to their total numbers though their relative significance is decreasing.[1]

Deterioration of the human kind through excessive fecundity of inferior strains is certainly a possibility that should be assiduously guarded against; it has not, however, been demonstrated to be a present reality.

Where inferiority of a non-heritable type is concerned, the need is for individual care and rehabilitation. Non-heritable inferiority is in general the result of ignorant rearing, neglect, poverty, bad feeding and the like. Where inferiority is heritable, there is presented to society not only the problem of the individuals in question but of their possible progeny. The apparent solution is to check propagation by sterilization, by the prevention or restriction of marriage — or possibly by education. The segregation of hereditary defectives in institutions and colonies has often been practiced or advocated. It is not fully effective however, because only pronounced cases are provided for, and these, we recall, are not the ones who propagate with dangerous rapidity. That society should permit the marriage of defectives and heritably diseased persons, and the church

[1] *World Population Conference*, 1927, London, pp. 137, 141, 142, 148, 163, 219, 220, 337, 339.

preside over their union is evidence of how slightly the man kind has progressed in the solution of its population problems.

Just what constitutes inferiority and superiority is of course far from being apparent. Individual investigators draw lines and define classes with little regard for anything but prejudice.[1] Moreover, it is far from clear in just what degree inferiority and superiority are heritable and in what degree they are ground into, or drawn out of, the individual by the give-and-take of life. It is generally agreed, however, that fortunately-endowed parents will have, more often than not, gifted children. It is also generally agreed that there are in every population definite and persistent inferior strains. Conversely, the conjugation of superior parents is by no means a guarantee against mediocre or downright inferior offspring. That talented individuals have sprung from inferior or mediocre parents is too well known to require laboring here. [2]

Investigators experience a strong temptation to see rare but cloaked gifts in the ancestors of persons who have demonstrated their superiority. Descendants of these geniuses in turn frequently shine for generations in the reflected light of ancestors—though intelligent scrutiny would reveal in them no ray of superiority. As a matter of fact, the human race is made up entirely of two-legged animals—very much alike—and certainly not vastly different one from another, nor from their ancestors of twenty, fifty, or even of one hundred thousand years ago; greatest care must be taken therefore in classifying human beings for any purpose.

One ought not, however, to read into these pages a denial of progress: to the contrary, progress is specifically recog-

[1] *Population Problems*, New York, 1926 (Dublin, Ed'r), pp. 14-15.

[2] *World Population Conference*, 1927, London, pp. 199-200, 204; Newsholme, Sir A., *op. cit.*, p. 110.

nized as biologic necessity. Persistence, be it recalled, is conclusive evidence of progress. Individuals, types, ideas, institutions, societies, races, nations, species develop or perish. There is no perfectly poised state.

To resume: " What is necessary is to make it deeply and widely felt that it is both immoral and unpatriotic for the sound in mind and body to unduly limit the size of their families." [1] Possibly such propaganda paired with a program designed to prevent the proliferation of inferiority, would not only speed biologic progress in the human kind but produce a race capable of solving its population problems.

Progress, especially in recent centuries, shows an appearance of sprightliness that is entirely superficial. Cultural progress is often mistaken for biologic progress. Cultural and social progress are not biologic matters nor are they necessarily contingent upon race improvement — or, conversely, biologic improvement is not prerequisite to social and cultural advance. The recent swift spread and elaboration of civilization is chiefly a matter of communication and education. Physical and mental progress, at least within historic times, has been of course entirely negligible. The progress of the race has been cultural, and the irresistible conclusion is that its future course will be almost entirely along the same lines. If this be true — regardless of the actual direction given to biologic change by a differential birth rate—it is unfortunate that families and classes with the best environment, tradition and standards should produce a number of children smaller than those produced by families and classes less happily circumstanced. Traits transmitted by social contact far outnumber and are of greater significance than traits transmitted biologically. The Chinese child speaks Chinese, the Swedish child speaks Swedish,

[1] Darwin, Leonard, *Address Before the International Congress of Eugenics*, New York, 1921.

the child reared in an educated and well-to-do family usually develops habits of thought and action that are in the main useful, while such habits are infrequently attained by children born to poor and crude parents. Modern scientists do not agree, however, that " Talented individuals are probably about as numerous in the lower classes as elsewhere." [1] Nevertheless it is to an extent true that sex, race and class proscriptions create a fictitious appearance of superiority among vast numbers conventionally deemed superior, and who are in fact mediocre or downright inferior, and vice versa. Among the unhappily circumstanced, a talented person often has small chance of exhibiting superiority except in craftsmanship—and only locally. Whereas in classes to whom circumstance insures privilege, a person possessing no more than bare common sense may, by following cultural formulæ, attain to considerable distinction.

One shudders to think how narrowly Newton escaped being an unknown farmer, or Faraday an obscure bookbinder, or Pasteur a provincial tanner. In the history of the world there must have been many men of equal native endowments who missed the slender chance which came to these. We form the habit of thinking of great men as having appeared only at long intervals, and yet we know that great crises always discover great men. What does this mean but that the men are ready formed and that it requires only this extra stimulus to call them forth? To most of us heredity is kind—kinder than we know. The possibilities within us are great, but they rarely come to full epiphany. [2]

There need, however, be no confusion of pivotal facts. In sum, a differential birth rate exists, but its effect is completely offset, or rather, reversed, by the production of

[1] Reuter, E. B., *Population Problems*, Philadelphia, 1923, p. 328.

[2] Conklin, E. G., *Heredity and Environment in the Development of Men*, Princeton (N. J.) Univ. Press, 1925, pp. 474-5.

favorable variants in inferior classes and by a differential death rate that bears with extreme weight upon unfavorable variants in all classes—though the only proof that exists lies in the generally accepted opinions that (1) society replenishes itself from its lower layers and dies off at the top, and (2) *continued existence is itself conclusive evidence of progress.*

CHAPTER XIV

In Sum

THE more perfectly a species is adapted to survival, the lower is its rate of increase: though this law of Spencer's concerns only age-long, biologic change, many scholars have made the mistake of trying to apply it in studies of recent population growth. It is true that among the several classes in society, those having the greatest economic self-sufficiency show in general the lowest birth rate, but quite patently, that is a psycho-economic matter. Fecundity, virtually fixed for the human kind by the accidents of a period extending through thousands of generations, does not change notably in the overnight of a century. Low birth rates among the well-to-do are the result of a mental attitude plus the knowledge necessary to make that attitude effective.

It is entirely valid, however, to apply Malthus' law in explaining population growth during periods so recent and so brief—comparatively speaking—that biologic change could not possibly be brought in by way of explanation; for Malthus' principle is economic as well as biologic. The inescapable converse of the Malthusian proposition—life everywhere tends constantly to exceed the warrant for it—is that population will always and everywhere tend to increase with, and in proportion to, improvement in the conditions of existence. The unfavorable reactions of environment upon organisms are bettered in two ways. Biologic changes, structural changes, occur within the organism itself: from generation to generation down through the ages, the species is remoulded in accord with the Darwinian hypothesis of biologic progress, a process of internal adaptation. Also the organism makes improvements in its environment: the burrows that rabbits dig in the ground; the houses, railroads, hospitals and golf-links that men build for themselves: these may be called external adaptations. The circumstance that sets man off most conspicuously from other animals is of course the extraordinary amount and variety of his external adaptations to environment. But it makes no difference whether adaptation proceeds from internal adjustment of organism or external adjustment of environment or from both; in any case the net effect is more leeway for proliferation.

In discussing the mode of population growth one need not, however, give any slightest attention to internal or biologic adaptations, which require ages to take effect, for the principles of population growth are concerned only with the centuries that are passing. Attention may be centered solely upon external adaptations—that is, upon wealth. Thus do we come easily to a statement of the relationship that is fundamental in determining the mode of human increase: population tends to increase directly with wealth.

Have populations forever increased and diminished strictly in accord with this first rough generalization concerning population growth? Clearly, they have not. Wealth, in recent millenniums, in recent centuries, in recent years, has increased magically; population has surged forward at a pace terrifying to many persons, even to serious students of the population problem; but population expansion has at no time kept equal pace with expanding wealth.[1]

The mode of human increase is not fully described by the simple formula: populations increase directly with wealth (weal). There is something missing. Some further constricting influence has still to be taken into account. The

[1] Ely, R. T., *Outlines of Economics*, New York, 1908, p. 436.

expansion of life, or of population, is not checked internally; that is to say by decreasing fecundity. It is checked externally, by the rigors of existence. The whole meaning of wealth, viewed broadly, is in its amelioration of the rigors of life. Therefore if populations do not increase as fast as wealth, one is forced beyond escape to conclude either that the increase of wealth is not equally distributed, or that each individual requires or demands, on the average, a constantly larger share.

That wealth is not equally distributed is a fact that requires no emphasis. Nothing could be more apparent. In our Western civilization less than one per cent of the people own more than one-half of all wealth. This, however, is an ancient arrangement—so ancient that it need not be considered a constricting influence when comparing population changes during recent, or historical, periods. In searching for constricting influences upon population growth the unequal distribution of wealth may therefore be disregarded.

Quite as obvious, however, as the unequal distribution of wealth is the fact that, from century to century and from year to year, each individual demands and receives on the average a larger and larger share in the material good things of life. This progressive process has long been recognized. England's leading economist of the second quarter of the nineteenth century said: " As wealth increases, what were the luxuries of one generation become the decencies of their successors. Not only a taste for additional comfort and convenience, but a feeling of degradation in their absence, becomes more and more widely diffused." [1] The total supply of the material good things in life has increased enormously, but the share in it that each individual, on the average, demands and appropriates has increased even more rapidly.

[1] Senior, Nassau William, *Two Lectures on Population*, London, 1828, p. 7.

If population growth, past, present and future, is dominated by the relationship between numbers and wealth, it is wholly apparent that human increase must be adversely affected by an increase in the share of wealth demanded and received by each individual, that is, by increasing living standards. Thus we come to our complete formula, or hypothesis, of the mode of human increase: In a capitalistic civilization, population size tends to vary directly with the aggregate supply of wealth and inversely with the height of the prevailing standard of living.

In satisfying one's wants, attention is divided between necessaries and ego-titivating or ego-fattening comforts and luxuries. The proportion of attention devoted to replenishing the body and replenishing the ego varies from one economic class to another. The highest economic classes need give comparatively little attention to physical threats and wants: the greater portion of income in these classes is devoted to activities and accessories that enhance self-esteem rather than welfare. The poorest classes, on the other hand, must devote all energy to securing the starkest rudiments of life; the slightest deviation into the field of principally ego-soothing activities and attitudes beckons disaster.

Struck by the magic development of our capitalistic Western civilization many scholars, writers and conspicuous men of more material interest have assured us that one economic class after another has escaped the competition to persist: finally, in the most progressive nations, all classes have clambered above the reach of raw necessity. This is not true. Machinery and political and economic democracy have combined to enlarge and constantly increase the proportion of persons living in a somewhat self-satisfying way and to reduce sharply the number who must bend all energy to flopping hopelessly back and forth from frying-pan to fire. In the more progressive states of Western civilization—Canada, United States, New Zealand, and Australia—the number of persons living in poverty has been reduced to include scarcely more than the patently under-endowed. This group is small in proportion to the totals of modern populations, but it is not inconsiderable. Because of its relatively smaller size, and because it hides its shame in back streets, many intelligent, influential persons are convinced that this group no longer exists.

The framework of the population problem is a social organization shaped almost exclusively for the production and consumption of wealth. In its boldest features it shows a simple stratification of classes distinguished principally by the scope of their command over the material good things of life; the scope of this command is in turn roughly proportioned to the fruitfulness and rarity of the type of productive ability possessed by each individual or organized group. Economic and political democracy permits a surprisingly extensive migration of individuals from one economic stratum to another; and around the possibility of shifting from class to class has grown up the tradition that every person should strive to reach a higher economic class. This curious rule of conduct quite naturally makes its strongest appeal to those who happen to possess characters shaped for success in the established order of society. The 'desire for this sort of success, economic success—the desire for higher standards of living—increases therefore, and increases cumulatively, from class to class upward in the economic scale.

Niceforo holds a pertinent opinion: " During our period, production and wealth have increased . . . (but) new wants have arisen faster. It is these ever-increasing desires that determine the number of births. . . . Wants increase and multiply faster than wealth." [1] Professor Carr-Saunders concurs: " The fact that the upper social classes began to

[1] *World Population Conference* (Proceedings), London, 1927, p. 66.

restrict their increase before the lower social classes is partly due to the fact that they are more sensitive to economic requirements." [2]

Within the lowest class one finds a considerable amount of compelling evidence to show that the desire for a higher plane of living amounts to almost nothing. Upward from class to class the striving for ever higher living standards becomes constantly more strenuous. The facts evidencing this phenomenon suggest that it is partly a matter of individual constitution and partly a matter of education (in the broadest sense). The modern view is that it is most significantly a matter of awareness and that awareness is more a matter of experience than endowment. The person born to the meanest squalor usually surrenders abjectly. He never sees beyond the limits of his class—until too late for anything but despair or frenzy. He does not believe in the possibility of a reliably better existence — at least not for himself and his fellows. His environment schools him, or anesthetizes him, to something very like satisfaction with his surroundings. But with accidental experience or second-hand experience (attendance at the cinema, for example) becoming daily more likely—experience pricking ambition, and satisfied ambition opening the way to new experience—wants pile up prodigiously, and we have a complete explanation of the cumulative nature of the desire for higher and ever higher standards of living.

If the amount of wealth available at a given time is limited, and if an individual's ability to acquire for himself and for his family the largest possible share in that wealth is also limited, the most promising point of flexibility in the ambition-thwarting circumstances of his existence is family size, that is to say, the number of shares into which the wealth he is able to acquire must be split. That, and that

[1] *The Population Problem*, Oxford, 1922, p. 308.

alone, may be regulated—a fact which does not long remain obscure to educated persons of some intelligence. Herein lies the explanation of the steady decrease in family size, or birth rate, as wealth, experience and education increase— whether we speak of individuals, of nations or of races. Be it remembered, furthermore, that experience and education, even in the most democratic nations, are simply two of the things into which wealth may be converted. The indifference of the shiftless negro to the size of his brood of children, and the prolificness of backward nations and races the world around find adequate explanation in their almost complete inhibition of desire for higher living standards.

In our present capitalistic society, therefore, in which distinction — ego-satisfying position — is so nicely correlated with wealth, population tends to vary inversely with the height of living standards. Or, as one notably moral reviewer of Senior's Oxford Lectures of 1828 quaintly phrased it : " More persons will rather dine alone on champagne and chickens than share their roast beef and pudding with a wife and family."

Briefly, population growth is governed by birth rates and death rates. Above the theoretical minimum, death rates are controlled by factors which are in turn determined by the supply of wealth. Economic conditions constitute the immediate limitation that everywhere prevents or retards a lowering of death rates to the theoretical minimum—especially in this day of highly organized and costly methods of education, research and practice in medicine, surgery and hygiene. Birth rates are controlled by intelligence and education, which in general determines the strength of the desire for ever higher standards of living. It is not to be contended for an instant that high standards of living repress directly the growth of populations: it is the *desire* for higher living-standards that exercise a repressive effect. But the *desire* for higher living-standards rises with a rise in living-standards, and, since it is impossible to measure *desire* directly, and because it can be measured with considerable precision by the height of living-standards, our complete formula runs: *population size tends to vary directly with aggregate wealth, and inversely with the height of standards of living.*

The ideas contained in this formula are not entirely original — not even the second clause — at least, statements very much like them appear again and again in the literature of population, economics and biology. As with the famous Malthusian and Darwinian propositions the development of this slight hypothesis is mainly a matter of synthesis. Our formula, moreover, is quite plainly circuitous; but the central, the essential, the key thought in the Darwinian hypothesis of progress and the Malthusian law of poverty (and in all sound natural law) follows a circuitous path: in fact it is the very circuitousness of the process pursued in the development of natural law which leaves the unmistakable impression of law.

The first clause of our principle of population growth is, we repeat, simply the converse of the oldest and most respectable of biologic axioms. One cannot offer completely satisfying evidence of the truth of the second clause, because here one deals with a psychological process, a psycho-economic force, and it is impossible to isolate and measure precisely each given cause and predicted effect. One can do little more than point to the fact that in low-birth-rate nations living standards are high, and in high-birth-rate nations each individual has, on the average, a pitifully small amount of the material good things of life. Further evidence is presented in the smaller families of persons who are capable of securing high standards of material existence, and who crave even higher standards; Professor Pearl gives some arresting figures:

THE ECONOMIC ASPECT OF THE DIFFERENTIAL BIRTH RATE
IN THE UNITED STATES

Per Capita Wealth ...	$4,417	$3,838	$3,145	$2,991	$2,822	$1,840
Birth Rate	33.2	36.0	41.2	45.3	50.0	60.5

Pearl, R., *Problems of Over-Population* (M. Sanger, Ed'r), New York, 1926, p. 22.

For further substantiation of the second clause of our formula, recent statements of four notably careful scholars are available: " Each family wishes to rise in the social scale; and many parents believe that only through rigidly limiting the size of their families can they give its individual members opportunities for advancement." [1] "The declining birth rate . . . is not caused by greater stress in modern life, but is a consequence of the greater desire for luxury." [2] " It is these ever-increasing desires that determine the number of births." [3] " The declining birth rate . . . is an expression fundamentally and ultimately of economic influences." [4]

Ricardo's parallel statement has been quoted. Bastiat expressed the hope " that workmen's standards of living may rise so that their numbers shall increase less rapidly." John Stuart Mill maintained that with the coming of democracy and widespread education, new standards of living would be formed and that the increase of mankind would be thereby limited. [5] More recently, Lewis H. Haney speaks of " education and prudence " in connection with " the power of the

[1] Dublin, L. I., *Population Problems*, New York, 1926, pp. 240-241.

[2] Newsholme, A. and Stevenson, *Journal of Royal Statistical Society*, vol. lxix, pt. i, p. 8.

[3] Niceforo, A., *Proceedings of the World Population Conference*, London, 1927, p. 66.

[4] Sweeney, J. S., *The Natural Increase of Mankind*, Baltimore, 1926, p. 33.

[5] *Principles of Economics*, book ii, chapter iii.

standard of living above subsistence " to repress the growth of population.[1] Tandler holds that " The moment when the sense of responsibility for children enters the consciousness of the parent, pure instinct has reached its end and intelligence enters. Foresight in regard to economic conditions now becomes the controlling cause. . . . Wholly instinctive reproduction remains only amongst the irresponsible, the anti-social and the degenerate.' [2]

" The declining birth rate, as far as our evidence goes, is in the main produced by the practice of birth control, and *is an expression fundamentally and ultimately of economic influences* " : once more, the voice of Professor Pearl's pupil, Doctor Sweeney.[3] MacIver says, "The fall in the birth rate is an outcome of human psychology." [4]   N. W. Senior, England's great economist of a century ago, laid down " the four elementary propositions of the science of political economy "; Senior's second axiom was, " Population is limited only by moral and physical evils and by the standard of living." [5]

In East's book there is a sentence that concurs almost exactly with our full formula—both clauses, here indicated by (a) and (b) : (a) " Efficient labor, less waste, and better distribution will indeed provide for a greater population (b) under a given standard of living." [6]   Finally, Malthus himself: (a) " Population invariably increases where the means of subsistence increase, (b) unless prevented by some

[1] Haney, L. H., *History of Economic Thought*, New York, 1924, p. 244.

[2] *World Population Conference* (Proceedings), London, 1927, p. 209.

[3] Sweeney, *op. cit.*, p. 33 (italics ours).

[4] *Population Problems* (L. I. Dublin, Ed'r), New York, 1926, p. 297.

[5] Senior, N. W., *Industrial Efficiency and Social Economy* (Levy, S. L., Ed'r), New York, 1928, p. 12.

[6] East, E. M., *Mankind at the Crossroads*, New York, 1923, p. 57.

very powerful and obvious checks." [1] We present, of course, as the "powerful and obvious check" birth control which, in general, operates in direct proportion to the *desire* for higher living standards.

In sum, the proposition submitted in these pages is as simple as this: If an airplane brings, each day, to a colony of one hundred persons isolated on an inaccessible and barren highland exactly enough food to sustain one hundred persons, then regardless of prolificness, government, religion, custom or any other matter, the propagating power and inclination of the human kind will provide a population of at least one hundred; the limited food supply will insure that there shall be no more. If the food carrier agrees to bring to this people certain comforts and luxuries, and in compensation they agree to suffer a reduction of one-half in their daily food supply, fifty persons must die — quietly or violently, as they prefer. Thenceforth, population will remain constantly at fifty. Of course, within these absolute limits there is room for the play of other than economic influences upon population growth—religion, law, tradition—but even in advanced nations of Western civilization, economic motives and ideals crowd all others in a very small corner of the "group mind".

In present-day economic and capitalistic societies, psycho-economic forces dominate population growth. Populations tend to increase as the supply of wealth increases and to decline with increases in the size of the shares into which that supply of wealth is split. To an extent, economic forces determine population growth directly, but to a far greater extent their effect is indirect—working through psychologic channels. Once more, the formula developed in this book cannot of course pretend to the universal and eternal appearance possessed by the first and second laws of thermo-

[1] *The Principle of Population*, 7th ed., I. ii. 12n.; 2nd ed., p. 16.

dynamics or any of the mathematically expressed laws of physics. Like Gresham's law and the relationships existing between supply, demand and price, it is true only for present-day capitalistic societies. To the extent that societies are non-capitalistic and non-economic our formula will show "leakage" and "slippage"—but the extent to which present-day societies have departed from capitalism and the extent to which their dominant motives are non-economic is very, very slight.

CHAPTER XV

In Prospect

ALL science is an estimate. All substance is composed of earth, air, fire or water. That is not true; but once it was true—so far as any science is ever true. At the time of its currency it was the most reasonable explanation of matter; no subsequent explanation can be affirmed in stronger terms. All matter is composed of indivisible, infinitesimal, ultimate particles called atoms. That is not true, but it was true— so far as science is ever true: we of the current generation sacrificed on that altar, burned our candles and mumbled the ritual: we believed the atomic explanation of matter because it was the most reasonable theory available. Is the current theory of matter true in any other sense of the word? Again, Newton's law of gravitation is not true; it is practicably true, but it is not perfectly true. (At least, that is what Einstein tells us.) All knowledge, all scientific law is merely the current estimate of things and their functioning—a temporary working agreement among experts: subject to amendment, at any point, the moment a new instrument or a new mind permits scientists to see further or more clearly.

A science or a scientific law is an explanation—valid in so far as it explains to the trained, better-than-average mind the relations and sequences occurring among the phenomena that come within its scope. Scientists occasionally pretend that a science or a scientific law has absolute or complete objective validity. But, by their own definition, objectivity is the trait of presenting the same aspect to all better-than-average, trained minds. Objectivity therefore means merely a rather low degree of subjectivity.

Does our proposition concerning population growth, *explain?* Beyond a doubt its first clause (which is the converse, we recall, of the first axiom of biology) is the most apt explanation of the spreading and proliferating of peoples. Does its second clause explain the very apparent constriction in the "natural" rate of population growth? Does it supersede, or include, all other satisfying explanations of the slowness of human increase—for example, does it supersede, or include, the Malthusian checks?

Although Malthus elaborated his checks upon population growth through six editions of his book, producing finally a special set of checks for each important nation, the fullest elaboration of his checks can, for practical purposes, be boiled down to (1) food scarcity, (2) disease, (3) violence, (4) vice, (5) abstention. Viewed through a vista of one hundred and fifty years it is not quite possible to say precisely what Malthus meant by " vice "; still it is reasonable to suppose that there could be no objection to including it, or its effect at any rate, in the general effect of " disease." The complete Malthusian proposition then may be stated thus: population increase tends always and everywhere to exceed the warrant for it, but it is checked by (1) food scarcity, (2) disease, (3) violence, and (4) abstention. Or, formulated more freely: Malthus found that population is capable of increasing at a rate far greater than any recorded in history, and that this tendency to grow at unheard-of rates is held in check by food scarcity, disease and violence—in so far as the effect of these is not anticipated by abstention. Now our proposition, stated simply, is that food scarcity, disease and violence have been so generally abated that there appears some promise of their gradually becoming curiosities in human experience. Therefore abstention—or rather its modern expression, voluntary parenthood—is shortly to assume almost complete control of population growth. (Voluntary parenthood is, moreover, the most effective influence in reducing food scarcity, disease and violence.)

Before going further, however, let us test the proposition advanced in these pages by comparing it with the ideas of a recognized authority, a man of international reputation, familiar with the literature of population, and expressing a strong, clear, middle-of-the-road view, Professor Edward Alsworth Ross. Ross ventures " a fresh attack " upon Malthus because his famous essay is no longer fit to guide us.[1] But at the outset, let us recite the proposition we are to test: Population everywhere and always tends to increase directly with wealth and inversely with the prevailing level of the standard of living. Professor Ross' attack takes the form of thirteen points all of which are cited below and commented upon in parentheses:

1. Malthus's " law " that population increases in a geometrical ratio whereas subsistence can be increased only in an arithmetical ratio was rejected long ago. What he was driving at is the economist's " law of diminishing returns." (Here Professor Ross sets up the usual straw-man Malthus, and of course knocks him flat.)

2. Malthus was stumped by the query why a benevolent God created us with a bent to multiply faster than we can enlarge our food supply. Today in the light of evolution we have no difficulty in seeing how this super-fecundity may have become established. (As both Darwin and Wallace acknowledge that they got the essence of their hypothesis from Malthus, this statement sounds like trying to harm a water fowl with water.)

3. In Malthus's day those too intelligent to regard epidemics as God's chastisements held to the filth theory of human disease.

---

[1] Ross, E. A., *Standing Room Only?*, New York, 1927, p. vi.

The germ theory has been ascendant no more than fifty years. (Quite true, but the discovery of " the germ theory " resulted in an amelioration of the conditions of existence—incidentally the effectiveness of this discovery is closely related to available wealth—and furnishes therefore merely additional explanation of population growth, whereas it is population construction that lacks adequate explanation. It might also be noted that filth carries germs.)

4. At the dawn of the nineteenth century when Malthus was writing, no one dreamed of victories over human ailments that would cut the death-rate to a half, even to a third. (This of course merely an extension of the idea contained in paragraph three.)

5. Malthus offered no means of keeping down numbers save the postponement of marriage. Contraceptive means of regulating family size lay in the womb of the future. (Many authorities can be cited for the opinion that contraceptive devices are at least as old as papyrus: descriptions of such devices, written upon papyrus by ancient Egyptians, have come down to us. However, was not Malthus, a priest in the established church and later an employee of a corporation school, acting wisely not to get himself unnecessarily into print on that subject? Though in his youth he campaigned with energy for birth control, the great John Stuart Mill was amazingly silent upon that subject in later years.[1]

6. Unable to imagine steamship and railroad Malthus could not foresee how his people would set their table with food from all over the globe and how famine would disappear from the horizon of civilized peoples. (Here again Professor Ross points out merely an amelioration of the rigors of life—warrant for an increased rate of population growth—and not an explanation of the point that needs explaining, the retardation of growth in numbers.)

7. Malthus conceived that England might " in the course of some centuries contain two or three times its present population

[1] Himes, N. E., " John Stuart Mill's Attitude Toward Neo-Malthusianism, *Econ. Jour'l.* (Supplement), January, 1929.

and yet every man in the Kingdom be much better fed and clothed than he is at present." Thanks to the new forces his people doubled in fifty years and again in the next sixty years, while their plane of living rose. (What can one see here but as neat, sane and conservative a piece of prophecy as is offered anywhere in the whole literature of moral philosophy or the social sciences? The fact that Malthus was slightly over-conservative in his prediction is not too discreditable.)

8. In his day no one foretold such facility of overseas move-ment that surplus people in the congested parts of the earth would migrate in vast streams toward the roomy, democratic, and well governed lands. (The net effect of migration is a very slight amelioration, the world over, of the conditions of existence. Here is merely an extension of the idea contained in paragraph 6.)

9. Since Malthus, much has been learned as to the possibili-ties of the limitations upon food production. (It is difficult to extract the meaning of this cryptic statement, but probably it can be taken at about its face value.)

10. Although he championed popular education, Malthus never dreamed of such a laboring population as we know today —ambitious and aspiring, reading newspapers and advertise-ments designed to breed in them new wants. (Here Professor Ross recognizes the psychological forces working in accord with the second clause of our hypothesis of population growth.)

11. Malthus did not foresee the development of democracy to such a point that in some countries the laboring class are practising prudence in the matter of family, not from dread of want, but from fear of losing the style of living essential to one's standing in the eyes of others and hence to one's self respect. (Again, Professor Ross simply presents an excellent statement of the forces working under the second clause of our rule of population growth.)

12. Malthus had no presentiment of women becoming so emancipated that their revolt against the needless anguish and mortality of excessive child-bearing would appreciably lower

the birth-rate. The emancipation of women has beyond a doubt been a tremendous influence in constricting population growth; but may not this be considered a purely incidental matter? Women emancipated are finally emancipated, and that particular influence upon population growth need not be considered again. The effect is like that of a sudden gust of air striking a tennis ball falling under the action of the law of gravitation; its speed and course is for a moment altered—but the law of graviation remains the same.)

13. Finally, Malthus could not foresee that the extension of the rule of the advanced nations over the backward would cause human life to be conserved among the blindly multiplying peoples of Asia and Africa with much of the intelligence and zeal with which it is conserved among the prudently multiplying peoples of Europe and America. (Again Professor Ross is speaking of an amelioration of the conditions of existence—for backward peoples—offering an explanation of population expansion which is fully explained by the first axiom of biology, but offering no explanation of the real enigma, the slowness of population growth.)

Professor Ross' summary, in thirteen points, of the orthodox modern view of population growth does not obliterate Malthus; and it expresses nothing—Malthusian or Neo-Malthusian—that is not included in our formula. At the same time its obscure, tenuous, lengthy thirteen propositions illustrate the need for a synthesis of population principles expressed in a clear-cut formula. If a scholar of Professor Ross' unsurpassed ability and international reputation can be so obscure when he is obviously making a painstaking effort to be concise and clear, a rough working formula of population growth should prove instructive to say the least. And here, once more, we should perhaps point out that our formula does not pretend to possess absolute mathematical integrity; it pretends only to offer a clear statement of the way in which population growth is related, directly and through psychological channels, to its obviously fundamental correlatives, wealth and its distributions.

Once more, be it said, the hypothesis presented in these pages is not new in its several parts; simply, it has never been presented as a single, unitary description of the mode of human increase in capitalistic societies. Of the immeasurably more important Malthusian hypothesis the *Edinburgh Review* says, " Disclaiming all pretentions to discovery he (Malthus) has aimed only at fixing the attention of mankind on the character of certain phenomena that have always been before their eyes." [1]

What major effects will the working of the principles expressed in our formula have upon future trends in population? Standards of living mount; high standards move outward in widening circles from class to class. The ideals of material existence entertained by advanced nations of Western civilization are voiced, for example, by the late president of the American Federation of Labor, Samuel Gompers, who maintained that every workman should own an automobile, an ideal which has been very nearly realized in the United States—As these ideals of material existence seep outward to the alleged backward peoples of the earth, we may safely conclude that these peoples make every effort to imitate, as nearly as they can, the higher living-standards. Thereupon, unless the boldly written experience in our Western Civilization during the last few decades is to count for nothing, the rate of proliferation of these peoples will fall off sharply. Since the term *backward peoples of the earth* is nearly coincident with *colored peoples of the earth*— yellow, black, red and brown—the ' rising tide of color ' [2]

[1] Vol. 16 (April-August, 1810), p. 466.

[2] Stoddard, Lothrop, *The Rising Tide of Color*, Charles Scribner's Son, New York, 1926.

will be stemmed and the " twilight of the white races " [1] will
at least be delayed.   The differential rate of proliferation in
favor of colored races—if it has not already been cancelled—
gives promise of being cancelled or reversed in the future.

Moreover, as appreciation of higher standards of material
welfare comes to the lower classes in our Western Civilization through the broadened range of experience made possible by low-priced automobiles, radio, talking pictures, tele-
vision, and universal painless education, and as these lower
classes gain familiarity with the more effective and less
obnoxious means of controlling family size, following an
abatement of anti-intelligence laws, the differential birth rate
in favor of infrior strains will also be reversed.

It is difficult to exaggerate the bitterness and energy with
which anti-intelligence activities are carried out by agencies
opposed to liberating the lower orders of mankind from the
biting lash of the whip of bare necessity.   These conserva-
tives, we recall, are recruited principally from the more conspicuously religious members of the community and from the
military party.   However, they form a very close phalanx
and the association is extremely ancient.   Military people are
often deeply religious, and religious people are sometimes
quite militant.   In the Middle Ages a great deal was heard of
Christian soldiers and of the armies of Christ; the cross and
the sword got so mixed up that swords were made in the
form of the cross, and the impress of the cross and the bless-
ings of the church were given to all implements of
destruction.

During one month of 1929, in the United States, which,
however, it is only fair to say is the most backward, in sex
education, among nations of western civilization, an eminent biologist, the head of one of the oldest and strongest

[1] Muret, M., *The Twilight of the White Races*, Charles Scribner's
Son, New York, 1926.

state universities was compelled to resign because, (among other faults) he did not believe that a discussion of the advantages and disadvantages of voluntary parenthood was vicious; the police of New York City entered forcibly the Birth Control Clinic, a charitable and law-abiding organization, dumped, destroyed or carried off confidential records and correspondence and arrested five members of the staff for distributing 'indecent' literature by mail; the Council for Social work in the city of Philadelphia (the fourth or fifth largest city in the World) passed a by-law *forbidding forever* discussion before that body of anything pertinent to birth control; two professors in one of the largest state universities in the United States were dismissed for distributing to students a questionnaire dealing, among other things, with birth control; in California a mechanic was sent to jail for three months for selling a pamphlet entitled " Family Limitation "—these incidents indicate the levels to which militant ignorance has risen in the United States.

But the sovereign, the incontrovertible proposition that flows from the materials of population study presented and examined in these pages is this: however rapid the present rate of decline in death rates—or however rapidly they may fall in future—they are beset, so far as science can determine, with a rather high absolute minimum. Below a certain point, death rates cannot fall. As they approach that point they will fall at an ever slower rate. On the other hand, the birth rate—*that* may conceivably drop to zero. Brisk rhetoric and poignant oratory has no power to jockey us around these two points: with a high material premium put upon the reduction of birth rates—which, be it remembered, may be reduced to zero—and with death rates absolutely irreducible beyond a certain rather high minimum, no matter how great the premium, the conclusion seems inescapable; the present decreasing rate of human increase will continue to dwindle until population growth comes to a full stop.

After population size reaches its maximum, in a not distant generation—a world population perhaps not far greater than the present total—it is possible that from that level numbers may actually decline. Final stabilization may take place at a level considerably lower than the present one.

In 1924, A. L. Bowley wrote: " With the present rates of births, deaths and emigration, the population of Great Britain should increase to forty-five or forty-six millions in about 1941 and then diminish." [1]   In fact as long ago as 1895 Cannan predicted precisely that condition.[2]   According to Alfred Sauvy, the population of France will attain its maximum in 1935; then it will diminish until it reaches 38,-023,000 in 1956.[3]   Kahn predicts that the German population will also reach its maximum in 1935, and then shrink until a total of only 46,000,000 remains in 1975.   In 1929 Dublin concluded that, " We are much nearer to the conditions for a stationary population than we had realized. . . . There is danger that the natural rate of increase of the American population may give place to a natural rate of decrease." [4]   Later, Dublin became more definite: " The continuation of the present tendency of rapid decline in the birth rate will in all probability result in bringing about a virtually stationary population in the United States by the year 1970.   And at that time, under present immigration restrictions, the population of the United States will be ap-

[1] Bowley, A. L., *The Economic Journal*, vol. 24, p. 192.

[2] Cannan, E., " The Probability of the Cessation of the Growth of Population," *Econ. Journal*, 1895, pp. 505 *et seq.*

[3] Jl. Soc. Stat. de Paris, Dec., 1928, *La Population Francaise jusqu'en* 1956.

[4] Dublin, L. I., *Statistical Bulletin* (Metropolitan Life Insurance Co., New York), vol. x, no. 7, p. 3.

proximately 150,000,000."[1] This is about twenty million less than the maximum predicted by Pearl and Reed for the year 2015.

Propagation beyond the warrant for it, the principal source of poverty and human anguish, will, it appears, be brought to an end.

Quoting Professor Pearl:

When the issue which is to determine human behavior is drawn between the present comfort, happiness and well-being of the reproducers on the one hand, and the indefinitely future welfare of society in general, or the race or state, on the other hand, he would seem indeed a simple minded, not to say fatuous, optimist who supposes that the latter will outweigh the former.[2]

Moreover this influence, which has thus far brought its restrictive effect to bear only upon the upper classes, will soon be operating upon the most *numerous* classes in society. It seems therefore, although authoritative and sonorous voices warn to the contrary, the populations of the earth will never proliferate and spread so extensively that the world will be threatened with universal hunger—Nor will the inhabitants of the world, for want of space, trample upon one another's toes.[3]

Will the approximate stabilization of world populations eliminate war? No. In that remote age when men were as scarce as tigers today, there was, even then, the gathering of new loot by violence, aggressive warfare—and the defending of old loot. Many thoughtful scholars are however of the opinion that the voluntary restriction of population growth would go far in minimizing the risk of war.

[1] *Statistical Bulletin*, Metropolitan Life Insurance Co., New York, January, 1930.

[2] *World Population Conference*, London, 1927, pp. 211-213.

[3] Compare Beveridge, Sir. W. H., Presidential Address (section F), *British Association* (Liverpool, Sept. 17, 1923).

Persons who retain some remnant of respect for the ancient meaning of the word *ought* will possibly fear that, birth control becoming universal, the biologic progress of the man kind will cease. Let us recall in rough outline the nature of biologic progress. Three distinct elements or factors appear: the first two factors, heredity and variation, form the framework of the progress scheme; but the third is the key factor, the dynamic factor: propagation beyond the means of existence.

Heredity, the tendency of individuals to resemble their progenitors, may well be considered the first fact of biologic progress, without which all would be senseless confusion. Were heredity however the sole fact of regeneration, each successive generation would be exactly like the preceding— in the same sense that one sheet of two-cent stamps is like another, printed from the same plate. But superposed, there is the fact of variation. Variation is the tendency in individuals toward difference, but always within the meaning of the term heredity.

When the idea of variation is added to the idea of heredity, we see the vehicle of biologic progress complete; but still there is no motor. Propagation beyond the means of existence—here is our motor. This is the dynamic of biologic progress.

Of course, it is not, in reality, so simple as this. The " forces " of heredity and environment, for example, are not separable, except in complete abstraction—no more are heredity and variation. In fact, these three, merged to form a new concept of heredity—heredity in a cosmic rather than a parental sense—may be the only hope for the survival of the term heredity in biologic language. There is a complicated interplay of chromosomes, cytoplasm and external accident that eludes the grasp of any term now in use. A certain egg is compelled by a force within to produce an individual of predetermined characteristics—that concept of heredity is outworn and discarded. It now means but little more than this: A certain frog egg is not predestined to become a frog of definite characteristics and markings, and a second frog to become an equally definite but slightly different frog. Simply, neither will ever become a canary— or even a hop toad. The main force of the term *heredity* is in negation.

Heredity insuring integrity, variation forming a basis for selection, and close-fisted Nature, acting through over-propagation, doing the selecting—this is the progress scheme, complete. Nature seizes the individual as he comes from the shaping hands of Heredity and Variation, and thrusts him, kicking, into an almost rigid mold, the conditions of existence. If he soon stops kicking and passes on to his reward, it is because he did not fit the conditions of existence. Others fit—and are called successful. They propagate, and Heredity shapes their offspring a little more to the mold, more on the average than were they and their non-fitting brothers, taken together—a millionth of a hair's breadth, perhaps.

No whit better than its actual progenitors, a generation is, nevertheless, a millionth of a hair's breadth better than the whole of the proceeding generation, misfits and fits lumped. Simply, the misfits perish before the time of propagation, or their children perish soon thereafter—in general only the more fit are reproduced. This is the natural method of progress; its price is constant struggle with no quarter given —merciless, wasteful destruction.

Following the spread and prevalence of birth control, progress of the sort just described will pass out of human life. Biologic progress will, however, be retained. From being, in all but general direction, a purely haphazard matter it will become in part the product of conscious policy. When a thorough understanding of contraceptive methods becomes substantially universal, those members of society who must struggle hardest to make a living will be the most reluctant to undertake what will then be the entirely optional responsibility of parenthood. Progress (biologic progress) will remain largely automatic, but it will be far more positive, sane and rapid.

From the opinion of Doctor Duncan and of Professor Carr-Saunders that modern women are capable, on the average, of bearing ten to twelve children and from the fact that the average number of children per marriage in our Western Civilization is slightly less than three [1]—and however bitter it may appear to persons absolutely opposed to voluntary parenthood—it seems impossible to escape the conclusion that birth control is today more nearly universal than either the telephone or automobile: in use it is more widely appreciated than the toothbrush.

Is the simple formula developed in these pages true for all times and for all societies? No. Manifestly, under a system of communism our formula would be meaningless; ownership and private property would be unknown; standards of living would be determined by the government; possibly marriage would be abolished; children would be cared for by the state. Under such a system it seems that proliferation would go on at a rate more horrifying than any the world has ever seen, for with everyone having an inalienable right to a living there would be no premium upon the limitation of family size; the state presumably would take care of all. Of course, heavy and progressive penalities might be put upon the bearing of children beyond the first and second or third. At any rate our formula would be meaningless in a communistic system, and its meaning would be impaired in any system which differed sharply from the sys-

[1] Carr-Saunders and Jones, *The Social Structure of England and Wales*, London, 1927, p. 12.

tem of private property and freedom of contract (the capitalistic system) which with steady but extremely slow modifications has formed the framework of the population problem from earliest times to the moment that is passing.[1]

One more question: Will general understanding of the principles expressed in this formula and a general knowledge of the means of counteracting the tendency toward over-population eliminate all forms of human misery? Clearly, no. Variation is a universal and ineradicable circumstance in regeneration; and so long as there is variation there will be unfavorable variants. These unfavorable variants, persons abnormal emotionally, mentally or physically, will be uncomfortable or downright miserable under any system. Furthermore, so long as the processes of human thought are uncertain there will be, in the structure and functioning of any social system, error and injustice. Friction will result, and friction will cause pain.

In prospect then, it appears that: (1) The growth of world population and of all population will soon halt; final stabilization may in any instance take place at a figure lower than the maximum numbers reached. (2) Present evidence points to the conclusion that the world will never face starvation on account of over-population. (3) Over-propagation in under-endowed classes is the source of modern poverty; poverty may be eliminated from human life. (4) There is every present indication that the white race will prevail. (5) Excepting brief periods and restricted areas, the ' dysgenic trend ' in birth rates has never been effective in lowering population quality; with universal birth control established the trend of the birth rate will not only lose its dysgenic appearance but will become pronouncedly eugenic; there will be a consequent speeding up of the biologic

[1] Present Author, " The Concept of Private Property," *Cornell Law Quarterly*, December, 1925.

progress of the human kind. (6) Population control is at present entirely haphazard but general in the Western Civilization; it will soon be everywhere officially recognized. (7) The systematic control of population growth—even the present automatic, psycho-economic control—will reduce, but will not eliminate, the possibility of war. (8) The discrepancy between reproductive capacity and the actual size of modern families is so great that influences upon the growth of population other than those prompting voluntary, rather than accidental, parenthood are entirely insignificant. (9) Future improvement in the technique of producing wealth will not be accompanied by an increase in population; hence the large probability is that leisure (merely, of course, one of the things into which wealth may be converted) and standards of living will reach levels unimagined.

In conclusion it may be stated (A) When applied to the growth of world population or to very large groups possessing the average intelligence and education current in the present Western Civilization, our hypothesis appears to have the force of law and the obviousness of discovered truism. (B) Within comparatively small selected groups, on the other hand, such as those ordinarily chosen to illustrate differential birth-rate trends, factors other than the psychoeconomic are, to a degree, in control, and until a technique of separating out these other influences is developed, our formula is not in such cases an entirely reliable criterion of interpretation.

AN HYPOTHESIS OF POPULATION GROWTH

List of Materials Used

Abbott, E., *Historical Aspects of the Immigration Problem*, University of Chicago Press, Chicago, 1926.

Adams, T. and Others, *Population, Land Values and Government*, New York, 1929.

Alison, A., *The Principles of Population*, London, 1840, 2 vols.

American Economic Review, " The Expansion of Europe in Population," 5:741-742.

American Public Health Association, "Health Officer's News Letter," vol. iv, no. 11.

Annals of Agriculture, Rev. of the New Publ'ns. Relating to Agriculture, Ed'n. of 1784.

Annals of American Academy, "Population, Migration and Race Rivalry," 112:113.

Ashby, A. W., " Population and the Land," *Edinburgh Review*, vol. 224, 1916.

Auerbach, F., " Law of Population Concentration," *Sci. Amer.*, Dec. 13, 1913.

Baber and Ross, " Changes in the Size of American Families in One Generation," *University of Wisconsin Studies*, 1924.

Baines, J. A., " The Recent Trend of Population in England and Wales," *Jour. Royal Stat. Soc.*, July, 1916.

Baldwin, B. T. and Roberts, *The Physical Growth of Children*, Iowa City, 1921.

Bear, F. E., " Food Problems of Tomorrow," *Paper read at Ohio State University*, 1929.

Beebe, W., *Edge of the Jungle*, New York, 1926.

Belleville-Yorkville, " Health Demonstration District, Analysis of Causes of Mortality and Morbidity," *Vital Statistics 1922-23-24*, October, 1926.

——, *Vital Statistics, 1925-26*, October, 1928.

Bernard, L. L., " Population and Social Progress," *J. Social Forces*, 3:21-30.

Beveridge, W. H., " Population and Unemployment," *Nature*, 112:458-50.

——, Presidential Address (Section F), *British Association*, Liverpool, 1923.

Blackwood Magazine (Letter from Thomas Doubleday), 41:374.

Bland, J. O. P., "Population and Food Supply," *Edinburgh Review*, 227 : 232-252, 247.

Blanshard, P., "How to Live on Forty-Six Cents a Day," *Nation*, 128 : 580.

Blodgett, J. H., "Relation of Population and Food Products in United States," *U. S. Agri. Bu. of Statistics*, 1903.

Blumner, H., *The Home Life of the Ancient Greeks*, Cassell and Co., New York, 1895.

Bodart, G., *Losses of Life in Modern Wars*, Austria-Hungary, France, London, 1918.

Bonar, J., *Malthus and His Work*, New York, 1924.

Bossard, J. H. S., *Problems of Social Well-Being*, New York, 1927.

Botsford, G. W., *Hellenic History*, New York, 1922.

Bowen, E., "Over-Population and Standard of Living," *Sci. Mo.*, 23 : 16.

——, "Progress—By Accident or Plan?" *Sci. Mo.*, vol. 20, Feb., 1925.

——, "A Sponge Theory of Population," *New Republic*, vol. xli, no. 527.

——, "The Concept of Private Property," *Cornell Law Quarterly*, December, 1925.

Bowen, F., "Malthusianism, Darwinism and Pessimism," *North American Review*, 129 : 447-472.

Bowley, A. L., "Births and Population in Great Britain," *Economic Journal*, 34 : 188-192.

——, "Estimates of the Working Population of Certain Countries in 1931 and 1941," *Publ'n League of Nations*, Geneva, 1926.

——, "Some Tests of the Trustworthiness of Public Statistics," *Economica*, No. 24, Dec., 1928.

Brend, W. A., *Health and the State*, London, 1920.

British Birth Rate Commission, Second Report, 1920.

Brooks, W. K., *The Oyster*, Johns Hopkins Press, Baltimore, 1891.

Brown, F. K., *The Life of William Godwin*, London, 1926.

Brown, F. G., "Land Rent as Function of Population Growth," *Sci. Mo.*, vol. 24, 1927.

Brown, F. W., "Fertility of Eugenic Middle Classes," *Eugenics Rev.*, 12 : 158-211.

Brunner, C. T., "Local Variations in the Birth Rate," *Econ. Jl.*, 35 : 60-5.

Bunle, H., "Relation entre les variations des indices economiques et le mouvement des mariages," *Jour. Soc. Statist.*, March, 1911.

Bushee, F. A., *Principles of Sociology*, New York, 1928.

Buxton, L. H. D., "Periodic Fluctuations in the Natural Increase in Man," *Eugenics Rev.*, 17 : 147-68.

Cairnes, J. E., *Character and Methods of Pol. Economics*, Lect. VII, second and enlarged edition, London, 1875.

Cannan, E., *History of the Theories of Production and Distribution from 1776-1848*, London, 1922, third edition.

——, "A Study in Malthusianism," *Econ. Jour.*, June, 1916.
——, *Wealth: A Brief Explanation of the Causes of Economic Welfare*, London, 1923.
Carr-Saunders, A. M., "Biology and War," *Foreign Affairs*, April, 1929.
——, *The Population Problem*, London, 1922.
Carr-Saunders & Jones, *The Social Structure of England and Wales*, London, 1927.
Cassel, G., *The Theory of Social Economy*, London, 1923.
Castle, W. E., "Can Selection Cause Genetic Change," *American Naturalist*, 50: 248-58.
Cattell, J. McKeen, "Families of American Men of Science," *Sci. Mo.*, 4: 248-262.
Chaddock, R. E., *Principles and Methods of Statistics*, New York, 1925.
Channing, E., *History of the United States*, New York, 1905.
Clement, E. H., "Counting China's Millions," *Harpers Weekly*, June, 1907.
Clement, H., *La Dépopulation en France*, Librairie Bloud et C., 1910.
Coats, R. H., "Growth of Population in Canada," *Ann. Am. Acad.*, 105 & 107: 1-7.
Cokkinis, A. J., *The Reproduction of Life*, New York, 1926.
Commerce Monthly, "Food Imports and Exports," National Bank of Commerce, N. Y., May, 1928.
Commons, J. R., *Races and Immigrants in America*, New York, 1920.
Conklin, E. G., *Heredity and Environment in the Development of Men*, Princeton (N. J.) Univ. Press, 1925.
——, *The Direction of Human Evolution*, New York, 1921.
Cook, S. A., *The Laws of Moses and the Code of Hammurabi*, London, 1903.
Cornell University Agricultural Experiment Station, Rural Population of New York, 1855 to 1925, Memoir 116, June, 1928.
Cornich, V., "Geographical Aspects of Eugenics," *Eugenics Rev.*, 16: 267-9.
Cox, H., "Population and Progress," *Edinburgh Rev.*, 232: 396.
——, *The Problem of Population*, New York, 1923.
——, "War and Population," *Edinburgh Review*, vol. 232, 1920.
Crackenthorpe, M., "Population and Progress," *Fortn.*, Dec., 1906.
Crum, F. S., "The Decadence of Native American Stock," *Quarterly Publn. Am. Stat. Assn.*, Sept., 1914.
——, "Marriage Rate in Massachusetts," *Am. Stat. Assn.*, Boston, 1897.
Darwin, C., *Descent of Man*, London, 1871.
——, *Life and Letters of Charles Darwin* (ed. by Francis Darwin), London, 1883.
——, *Origin of Species*, London, 1885.

——, *Variations of Animals and Plants Under Domestication*, New York, 1900.

Darwin, L., *Address Before the International Congress of Eugenics*, New York, 1921.

——, "Expenditure on Education and Its Effects on Fertility," *Eugenics Rev.*, 17 : 233-41.

——, "Some Birth Rate Problems," *Eugenics Rev.*, 12 : 147-57, 279-90.

——, "Some Observations on Fecundity," *Eugenics Rev.*, 14 : 266-9.

Das, T., *Religion and Ethical Aspects of Birth Control* (M. Sanger, Editor), New York, 1916.

Davenport, C. B., *Heredity in Relation to Eugenics*, New York, 1911.

Davis, W., "Earth's Population Limit," *Current History*, vol. 26, 1927.

Devine, E. T., *Misery and Its Causes*, New York, 1909.

Dickson, H. N., "Redistribution of Mankind," *Smithson-Rept.*, 1913.

Doubleday, T., *True Law of Population*, London, 1853.

Douglas, Hitchcock & Atkins, *The Worker in Modern Economic Society*, Chicago, 1923.

Douglas, P. H., *Real Wages in the U. S., 1890-1926*, N. Y., 1930.

Drysdale, C. V., "Birth Control and Eugenics in Holland," *Eugenics Rev.*, 15 : 472-9.

Dublin, L. I., "Factors in American Mortality," *American Econ. Rev.*, 6 : 526-548.

——, *Health and Wealth*, New York, 1928.

——, "The Mortality of Foreign Race Stocks, *Sci. Mo.*, 14 : 94-104.

——, (Editor), *Population Problems*, New York, 1926.

——, "Significance of the Declining Birthrate," *Science*, Feb. 1, 1918.

——, *Nineteenth Annual Meeting of the Tuberculosis Ass.*, 1923.

Dugdale, R. L., *The Jukes: A Study in Crime, Pauperism, Disease and Heredity*, New York, 1910.

Duncan, H. G., *Race and Population Problems*, New York, 1929.

Duncan, J. M., *Fecundity, Fertility and Sterility*, 2nd Edition (Edinburgh, 1871).

East, E. M., "The Agricultural Limits of Our Population," *Sci. Mo.*, 12 : 551-557.

——, *Heredity and Human Affairs*, New York, 1927.

——, *Mankind at the Crossroads*, New York, 1923.

——, "The Menace of Overpopulation, *The World's Work*, vol. xlx : 175-178, No. 2.

——, "Population," *Scientific Mo.*, 10 : 603-624.

——, "World Wide Problem of Over-Population," *Cur. History*, 24 : 523.

East and Jones, *Inbreeding and Outbreeding*, Philadelphia, 1919.

East Harlem Health Center, Births, Deaths, etc., Reports of 1921-27.

Edinburgh Review, vol. 64 : 469-506 and vol. 51 : 321.

Ellwood, C. A., *Sociology and Modern Social Problems* (rev. and enlarged edition), New York, 1913.

Ely, R. T., *Outlines of Economics*, New York, 1908.

Emerick, C. F., "The Diminishing Birth Rate Volition", *Popular Science Mo.*, 78: 71-80.

——, "A Neglected Factor in Race Suicide," *Pop. Sci. Quar.*, 25: 638-655.

Emerson, H., "War and Population," *Outlook*, vol. iii, 1915.

Encyclopedia Britannica (ed. of 1824), *MacVey Napier Supplement.*

Eugenics Review, "Working Men on Birth Conrtol," 15: 523-9.

Everett, A. H., "New Ideas on Population," *North American Rev.*, 17: 288-310.

Fairchild, H. E., *Applied Sociology*, New York, 1917.

Fairchild, H. P., *Immigration: A World Problem and its Significance*, 1925.

——, "The Paradox of Immigration," *Amer. Jour. Sociol.*, 17: 254-267.

Fetter, F. A., *Principles of Economics*, New York, 1911 (third edition).

Field, J. A., "Problems of Population After the War," *Am. Econ. Rev.*, 1917.

Fisher, I., "Birth Control," *Eugenics Rev.*, 13: 552-5.

——, *Introduction into Economics*, New York, 1910.

Franklin, B., *Observations Concerning Increase of Mankind*, New York, 1918.

Garnier, J., *Du Principe de Population*, Paris, 1757.

George, H., *Progress and Poverty*, new edition, New York, 1889.

Gibbons, H. De B., *Industry in England* (eighth ed. revised), London, 1902.

Giddings, F. H., *Principles of Sociology*, New York, 1921.

Gide, C., *Principles of Political Economy*, Boston, 1891.

Gide and Rist, *History of Economic Doctrines*, Boston, 1913.

Gillin, J. L., *Poverty and Dependency*, New York, 1921.

Gini, C., "Decline in the Birth Rate and The Fecundability of Woman," *Eugenics Rev.*, 17: 258-74.

Gini, C. and Others, *Population*, Chicago, 1930.

Goddard, H. H., *Feeble-Mindedness*, New York, 1914.

——, *The Kallekak Family*, New York, 1912.

Godwin, W., *Enquiry Concerning Political Justice*, London, 1793.

Goldenweiser, E. A., "Walker's Theory of Immigration," *Amer. Jour. Sociol.*, 17: 637-646.

Goltz, G., *La Solidarité de la Famille dans le droit criminal en Grèce*, Paris, 1924.

Gray, L. C., "Relation of Population, Land and Foreign Trade of U. S.," *Ann. Am. Acad.*, 112: 191-201.

Gregory, J. W., *Human Migration and the Future*, London, 1928.

Groves, E. R. and Osburn, W. F., *American Marriage and Family Relationship*, New York, 1928.

Gun, W. T. J., *Studies in Hereditary Ability*, London, 1928.

Haddon, A. C., *The Wanderings of Peoples*, Cambridge, England, 1912.
Hadley, A. T., "Population and Capital," *Publ. Amer. Econ. Asso.*, 9: 555-566.
——, *Economics*, New York, 1896.
Haekel, E., *The Evolution of Man*, New York, 1910.
Haire, N. (ed'r), *Some More Medical Views on Birth Control*, New York, 1928.
Haldane, J. B. S., "Eugenics and Social Reform," *New Republic*, 39: 119.
Hall, A. D., "Food and Population," *Edin. Rev.*, 244: 1926.
Hamilton, G. V. and McGowan, K., *What Is Wrong With Marriage*, 1929.
Haney, L. H., *History of Economic Thought*, New York, 1924.
Harris, J. A., "Variation, Correlation and Inheritance of Fertility In The Mammals," *Am. Naturalist*, 50: 626-36.
Hawley, F. B., *Capital and Population*, New York, 1902.
Hayes, E., "Significance of the Declining Birth Rate," *Science*, December 12, 1919.
Hazlitt, W., *New Writings* (collected by P. P. Howe), "Outlines of Political Economy," New York, 1927.
Hewes, A., "Factors in the Declining Birth-rate," *Am. Jour. Sociology*, Sept., 1916.
Hexter, H. B., "Implications of a Standard of Living," *Am. Jour. Sociology*, Sept., 1916.
——, *Social Consequences of Business Cycles*, New York, 1925.
Himes, N. E., "Charles Knowlton's Revolutionary Influence on the English Birth-rate," *New England Journ. of Medicine*, 199: 461-465.
——, A Critical Review of "Medical Aspects of Contraception," *New Journal of Medicine*, 200, 13-17.
——, "Eugenic Thought in the American Birth Control Movement 100 Years Ago," *Eugenics Rev.*, vol. ii, no. 5, 1929.
——, "John Stuart Mill's Attitude Toward Neo-Malthusianism," *Econ. Hist.*, 1: 457, no. 1.
——, "McCulloch's Relation to the Neo-Malthusian Propaganda of His Time," *Journal of Political Econ.*, vol. xxxvii, no. 1, Feb. 1929.
——, "Robert Dale Owen, The Pioneer of American Neo-Malthusianism," *Am. Jour. of Soc.*, vol. 35, no. 4.
——, "Some Untouched Birth Control Research Problems," *Eugenics*, vol. iii, no. 2, Feb., 1920.
Hollander, J. A., *Abolition of Poverty*, New York, 1914.
Hollingworth, L. S., "Social Devices for Impelling Women to Bear and Rear Children," *Amer. Jour. of Sociology*, 22: 19-29.
Holmes, S. J., *The Trend of the Race*, 1921.
——, "Will the Negro Survive in the North?" (Univ. of California Studies), *Sci. Mo.*, vol. 28, 1928, v. 27.

Homan, P. T., *Contemporary Economic Thought*, New York, 1928.

Houghteling, L., *The Income and Standard of Living of Unskilled Laborers in Chicago*, Univ. of Chicago Press, 1927.

Hourwich, L. A., "Immigration and Crime," *Amer. Jour. Sociol.*, 17: 478-490.

Hoyt, E. E., *The Consumption of Wealth*, New York, 1928.

Howlett, J., *An Examination of Dr. Price's Essay*, London, 1781.

Hume, D., *Political Essays* (The Populousness of Ancient Nations), London, 1752.

Hutchison, H. G., "World Congestion—Real Armageddon," *Quart. Rev.*, vol. 229, no. 453.

Huxley, J. S., "Late Fertilization and Sex Rate in Trout," *Nature*, 112: 828-9.

——, L., *Life and Letters of Thomas Henry Huxley*, New York, 1900.

Inge, W. R., "What Nations and Classes Do Prevail?" *Eugenics Rev.*, 11: 17-20.

Ingram, R. A., "Disquisitions on Population," *Edinburgh Rev.*, 16: 464-76.

James, E. W., "Malthusian Doctrine and the War," *Sci. Mo.*, 2: 260-272.

James, W., "Great Men, Great Thoughts, and the Environment," *Atl. Mo.*, 46: 441-459.

Jenks, J. W. and Lauch, W. J., *The Immigration Problem* (third edition), New York, 1922.

Jerome, H., *Migration and Business Cycles*, National Bureau of Economic Research, New York, 1926.

Johnson, A., "Are We in Danger of Over-Population?" *New Republic*, Nov. 21, 1923.

Johnston, H., *The Backward Peoples*, London, 1920.

Journal Soc. Stat. de Paris, "La Population Francaise jusqu'en 1956," December, 1928.

Keane, A. H., *Man: Past and Present*, Cambridge, Univ. Press, 1899.

Kellor, F., *Immigration and the Future*, New York, 1920.

Keith, A., *The Antiquity of Man*, Philadelphia, 1915.

Kelso, R. W., *Poverty*, New York, 1929.

Keynes, J. M., "Is Britain Over Populated?" *New Republic*, Oct. 31, 1923.

——, *The Economic Consequences of Peace*, New York, 1920.

Knibbs, G. H., *The Shadow of the World's Future*, London, 1928.

——, "The Menace of Increasing Population," *Sci. Mo.*, vol. 84, Oct., 1928.

Koster, M. S., *The Family of Sam Sixty*, Columbus Ohio Bd. of Administration, 1916.

Krieger, F., *Die Menstruation*, Berlin, 1869.

Kuczynski, R. R., *The Balance of Births and Deaths*, New York, 1928.

Leroy-Beaulieu, P., *La Question de La Population*, Paris, 1913.

Levasseur, P. E., *La Population Francaise*, Paris, 1889-1892.

Lewis, C. J. and J. N., *Natality and Fecundity*, Edinburgh, 1906.

Living Age, "War and Population," vol. 296, 1918.

Loeb, L., "Disease and Heredity," *Sci. Mo.*, 16: 54-587.

Lotka, A. J., "Sterility in American Marriages," *Nat. Acad. Sci. of U. S. of America*, 14: 99-109.

MacCurdy, G. G., *Human Origin*, New York, 1924.

MacIver, R. M., "Civilization and Population," *New Republic*, December 2, 1925.

Malthus, T. R., *Essay on the Principle of Population*, New York, 1923.

——, *Parallel Chapters From the 1st and 2nd Edition on the Principle of Population*, New York, 1895.

Marshall, A., *Principles of Economics*, New York, 1895.

Marshall, F. N., "Corpus Luteum and the Cause of Birth," *Nature*, 122: 242.

——, *Physiology of Reproduction* (2nd Ed'n), London, 1922.

Marshall, T. E., "The Population Problem During the Industrial Revolution," *Econ. Hist.*, 1: 457.

Martin, G. W., "The Food Resources of the Sea," *Sci. Mo.*, 15: 455-67.

Mayo-Smith, R., *Emigration and Immigration*, New York, 1904.

McDougall, W., *Is American Safe for Democracy?* New York, 1920.

McFall, R. J., "Factors Limiting Expansion of Human Race," *Ann. Am. Acad.*, vol. 112, 1924.

——, "Is Food the Limiting Factor in Population Growth?" *Yale Rev.*, 15: 297-316.

Meek, A., "Environment and Reproduction," *Nature*, 106: 532-3.

Mendel, L. B., *Nutrition*, Yale University Press, 1923.

Mendelsohn, S., *Saturated Civilization*, New York, 1926.

Meyer (et. al.), *Birth Control: Facts and Responsibility*, Baltimore, 1927.

Michel, A., "Population Pressure in Europe and Asia," *Liv. Age*, 317: 267.

Mill, J. S., *Principles of Economics*, New York, 1896.

Miller, K., "Enumeration Errors in Negro Population," *Sci. Mo.*, 14: 168-177.

Minot, C. S., *Age, Growth and Death*, New York, 1908.

Money, L. C. and Robbins, L., "Race and Population," *Outlook* (London), 56: 225-6.

——, *Peril of the White Race*, London, 1925.

More, T., *Utopia*, London, 1869.

Morimoto, Kokichi, *The Standard of Living in Japan*, Johns Hopkins University Studies, series xxxvi, no. 1.

Mudge, "Menace to the Eugenic race and to Its Traditions of Present Day Immigration and Emigration," *Eugenics Rev.*, 11: 202-12.

Mun, T., *England's Treasure in Foreign Trade*.

Muret, M., *The Twilight of the White Races*, New York, 1926.
National Council of Public Morals, "Report of National Birth Rate Commission, The Declining Birthrate (Its Causes and Effects), London, 1916.
———, Second Report, National Birth Rate Commission, Problems of Population and Parenthood, London, 1918-1920.
National Industrial Conf. Board: "The Cost of Living in Foreign Countries," New York, 1927.
———, "Cost of Living in New York City," New York, 1926.
———, "Cost of Living in the U. S. in 1914-1927," New York, 1928.
———, "Cost of Living in the U. S. in 1928," New York, 1929.
———, "The Immigration Problem," Report No. 58, New York, 1923.
Nature, "Causes of Fluctuations in Birth-rate," 108: 105-6.
———, "Population and Longevity," 113: 322-3.
———, "Reproduction, Lactation and Vitamin E.," 122: 136-8.
Nearing, S., "Race Suicide *v.* Overpopulation," *Pop. Sci. Mo.*, 78: 81-83.
Newsholme and Stevenson, "A National System of Notification and Registration of Sickness," *Jour. Roy. Stat. Soc.*, vol. 59.
Newsholme, A., *Vital Statistics*, 1924.
Nitti, F. S., *Population and the Social System*, New York, 1902.
North American Review, "The Laws of Population and Wages," 32: 1-28.
Norton, H. K., "Back of War ... Too Many People as a Cause," *World's Work*, April, 1928.
Orth, S. P., *Our Foreigners*, New Haven, 1920.
Orchard, J. F., "The Pressure of Population in Japan," *Geo. Rev.*, vol. 18, 1928.
Osborn, H. F., *Men of the Old Stone Age*, New York, 1915.
———, *The Origin and Evolution of Life*, New York, 1917.
Osborn, T. B. and Mendel, L. B., *Feeding Experiments With Isolated Food—Substances*, Washington, 1911.
Palgrave, R. H., *A Dictionary of Political Economy*, London, 1925-26.
Panunzio, C., *Immigration Crossroads*, New York, 1927.
Parmelee, M., *Poverty and Social Progress*, New York, 1917.
Patten, S. N., *Essays in Economic Theory*, New York, 1924.
———, *Development of English Thought*, New York, 1899.
———, *The New Basis of Civilization*, New York, 1907.
Patterson, E. M., *Europe in 1927: An Economic Survey*, Phila., 1927.
Patton, S. N., *Malthus and Ricardo*, New York, 1889.
Pearl, R., *The Biology of Population Growth*, New York, 1925.
———, *Biology of Death*, Philadelphia, 1922.
———, "Effect of War on the Chief Factors of Population Change," *Science*, n. s. 51: 553-56.
———, "Fecundity in the Domestic Fowl and the Selection Problem," *American Naturalist*, 50: 89-105.

——, " Further Note on the Age Index of a Population," *Nat. Acad. Sci. Prog.*, 8 : 300-3.

——, " Further Note on Mathematical Theory of Population Growth," *Nat. Acad. Sci. Prog.*, 8 : 365-8.

——, " Indigenous Native Population of Algeria in 1926," *Science*, vol. 65, D. C., 1927.

Pearl, R. and Parker, " On the Influence of Density on Population Upon the Rate of Reproduction in Drosophila," *Nat. Acad. Sci. Prog.*, 8 : 212-19.

——, *Rate of Living*, New York, 1928.

——, " Seasonal Fluctuations of the Vital Index of a Population," *Proceedings of Natl. Acad. Sci.*, 8 : 76.

——, *Studies in Human Biology*, Baltimore, 1924.

Pearl, R. and Burger, M. H., " The Vital Index of the Population of England and Wales," *Proceedings of Natl. Acad. Science*, 8 : 71.

Pell, C. E., *The Law of Births and Deaths*, London, 1921.

Peixotto, J. B., *Getting and Spending at the Professional Standard of Living*, New York, 1927.

Pennsylvania State Dept. of Health: Vital Statistics Bulletin, vol. iv, nos. 1, 2, 6 and 12, vol. v, no. 1.

Petty, W., *Political Arithmetic, Treatise of Taxes and Contribution*, edition of 1755.

Phillips, J. B., " The Declining Birth Rate," *University of Colorado Studies*, 7 : 159-178.

Pierson, N. G., *Principles of Economics*, New York, 1913.

Pinfield, F. C., " France and Her Vanishing Population," *No. Am. Rev.*, 188 : 682.

Pomeroy, H. S., *Is Man Too Prolific?*, New York, 1889.

Popenoe, R. and Johnson, R. H., *Applied Eugenics*, New York, 1918.

Pultney, I., *Problem of the Birth Rate*, London, 1920.

Rae, J., " Letters of Rae to Mill on the Malthusian Doctrine of Population," *Econ. Jour.*, 12 : 111-120.

Ragozin, Z. A., *Media, Babylon and Persia*, New York, 1888.

Raleigh, W., *Doctrine Upon War in General*, Oxford Press.

Rathbone, E. F., " Family Endowment in its Bearing on the Question of Population; with discussion," *Eugenics Rev.*, 16 : 270-84.

Reed, L. J. and Pearl, R., " Summation of Logistic Curves," *Roy. Stat. Soc. Jour.*, 4 : 729-46.

Reid, H, " Voluntary Parenthood," *Eugenics Rev.*, 12 : 29-31.

Registrar-General for England and Wales, Report of (Quarter ending Dec., 1928) and 1929.

Reuter, E., *Population Problems*, Philadelphia, 1923.

——, The Superiority of the Mulatto," *Amer. Jour. Sociol.*, 23 : 83-106.

Rew, H., " Food Resources of the World," *Edinburgh Rev.*, vol. 240, 1924.

Ricardo, D., *Principles of Economics*, New York, 1912.

Robbins, L., "Notes on Some Probable Consequences of the Advent of a Stationary Population in Great Britain," *Economica*, No. 25, April, 1929.

Roberts, L. J., *Nutrition Work With Children*, Chicago, 1927.

Robertson, J. M., *Economics of Progress*, London, 1918.

Rogers, A. G. L., *The Industrial and Commercial History of England*, London.

Round Table, "Birth Rate and the British Commonwealth," 18:777-97.

Roscher, W., *Political Economy*, Chicago, 1878.

Ross, E. A., *Foundations of Sociology*, New York, 1905.

——, *The Old World in the New*, New York, 1914.

——, *Standing Room Only?*, New York, 1927.

——, *World Drift*, New York, 1928.

——, "How Fast Can Man Increase?", *Sci. Mo.*, 24:263-67.

——, *Population Pressure and War*, 82:357.

Rossiter, W. S., "Pressure of Population," *Atlan. Mo.*, 108:836-43.

Rostovtzeff, M. I., *A History of the Ancient World*, 1926.

Rowntree, W. S., *Poverty*, New York.

Sadler, M. T., *Ireland: Its Evils and Their Remedies*, London, 1828.

——, *The Law of Population*, London, 1840.

Sanger, M. (Ed'r), *Problems of Over-population*, New York, 1926.

——, *Proceedings, World Population Conference*, London, 1927.

Schiller, F. C. S., "Ruin of Rome and Its Lessons to Us," *Eugenics Rev.*

Schlesinger, A. M., "The Significance of Immigration in American History," *Amer. Jour. Sociol.*, 27:71-85.

Schwiedland, E., "La Population au point de vue economique," *Rev. d'Econ Po.*, Jan.-Feb., 1911.

Science, "Growth of Population," vol. 65, Feb., 1927.

——, "Population," 67:339.

——, "Population of the U. S.," 57, No. 1469.

Sci. Monthly, "Foreign Born and Negro Population of U. S.," 10:284-87.

Seligman, E. R. A., *Principles of Economics*, New York, 1923.

Senior, N. W., *Two Lectures on Population*, London (reprinted 1928).

——, *Industrial Efficiency and Social Economy*, New York, 1928.

——, "Population and Emigration," *Quarterly Rev.*, 45:97-145.

Siegel, P. W., *Gewollte und Ungewolle Schwank unrgen der Weiblichen Fructbarkeit*, Berlin, 1917.

Small, A. W., *The Cameralists*, 1909.

Smith, A., *Wealth of Nations*, New York (reprinted 1924).

Smith, J. R., *The World's Food Resources*, New York, 1913.

Smith, P., *The Age of Reformation*, New York, 1920.

Spalding, H. S., "Ethics and the Neo-Malthusianism," *Am. J. Sec.*, vol. 22, March, 1917.

Spencer, H., *Principles of Biology*, New York, 1897.

——, *Theory of Population*, New York, 1905.

Spender, J. A., "Population and Agriculture," *Fortn.*, vol. 38, 1906.

Statistical Bulletin, "Metropolitan Life Insurance Co.," 5 : 12, 10 : 3, 10 : 7, 11 : 1.

Stangeland, C. E., *Pre-Malthusian Doctrines*, Columbia Univ. Press, New York, 1904.

Stephen, L., *English Utilitarians*, London, 1900.

Stoddard, L., *The Rising Tide of Color*, New York, 1926.

Sutherland, H. G., *Birth Control—Christian v. Malthusian Doctrine*, New York, 1922.

Sweeney, J. S., *The Natural Increase of Mankind*, Baltimore, 1926.

——, *The Population Problem*, Baltimore, 1926.

Swineburne, J., *Population and the Social Problem*, London, 1924.

Taussig, F. W., *Principles of Economics*, New York, 1918.

Taylor, H., "Senior's Social Economics," *Political Sci. Quar.*, vol. xliv, no. 1, March, 1929.

Temple, W., "An Essay upon the Advancement of Trade in Ireland," *Works* (1757 ed.).

Tenney, A. A., *Social Democracy and Population*, Columbia Univ. Press, New York, 1907.

Thomas, D. S., *Social Aspects of the Business Cycle*, New York, 1927.

Thomson, J. A., *Concerning Evolution*, 1925.

Thompson, R. E., *Political Economy*, Philadelphia, 1882.

Thompson, W. S., *Population Problems*, New York, 1930.

——, *Population—Study in Malthusianism*, Columbia Univ. Press, New York, 1915.

Thornton, W. T., "Overpopulation and its Remedy," *Edin Rev.*, 85 : 161-178.

Tucker, R. S., "Old Americans in 1920," *Q. J. Econ.*, vol. 37, August, 1923.

Tylor, W. R., "Increase of Contemporary Peoples," *No. Am. Rev.*, 218 : 607.

U. S. Dept. of Agriculture, "Changes in Farm Population," Feb. 13, 1929.

——, "Population, Food Supply and American Agriculture," *Geo. Rev.*, 18 : 353-373.

U. S. Dept. of Commerce, Bureau of Census, "Birth, Stillbirth, and Infant Mortality Statistics," 1925, 1926, 1927.

——, "Bureau of Census, A Century of Population Growth," 1910.

——, "Bureau of Census, U. S. Census of 1920," vol. ii.

——, "Bureau of Census, Estimates of Population of The U. S.," 1910-1923.

——, " Mortality Statistics," 1926 (part ii).

——, " Bureau of Census, Negro Population in the U. S., 1790-1915," 1918.

——, " Photo-stat of Current Records," Jan., 1929.

——, " Photo-stat of Vital Statistics of Registration Areas in the U. S.," 1926-27.

——, " Bureau of Census, Population," 1920, 1922.

——, " Special Report," Dec. 21, 1928.

U. S. Dept. of Labor, " Casual Factors in Infant Mortality," Bureau Publ'n No. 142, 1926.

——, " Infant Mortality " (Study, Akron, Ohio), Bu. Publn, No. 72, 1920.

——, " Infant Mortality," Bureau Publn. No. 119.

——, " Infant Mortality (Study, Gary, Ind.), Bu. Pub. 112, 1923.

——, " Infant Mortality " (Study, Johnstown, Pa.), Bu. Publn. No. 8, 1915.

——, " Infant Mortality " (Study, New Bedford, Mass.), Bu. Publn. No. 68, 1920.

——, " Infant Mortality and Proventative Work in New Zealand," Bu. Publn. No. 105, 1922.

——, " The Nutrition and Care of Children," Bu. Publn. No. 110, 1922.

——, " What is Malnutrition? ", Bu. Publn. No. 59, 1927.

U. S. Public Health Reports, Publ'n No. 47, vol. xxxiii, Nov., 1918.

United Hospital Fund of New York, Special Report, Jan 21, 1929.

University of California Publication, " Age at Parenthood, Order of Birth, and Parental Longevity in Relation to the Longevity of Offspring," 1928.

——, " Marriage Selection and Scholarship " (extract), 1927.

——, " The Approaching Extinction of the Mayflower Descendants " (extract), 1918.

Walker, F. A., Political Economy (2nd edition rev. and enlarged), New York, 1887.

——, " Immigration and Degradation," Forum, 11 : 634-644.

——, " Restriction of Immigration," Atl. Mo., 77 : 822-829.

——, Forum, August, 1911, vol. 11.

Wallace, A. R., My Life, New York, 1905.

Wattal, P. K., " Population Problem in India," Bombay, 1916.

Webb, S., " Physical Degeneracy or Race Suicide," Pop. Sci. Mo., 69 : 512-592.

Weber, A. F., " Growth of Cities in Nineteenth Century," New York, 1899.

Westminster Rev., " A Theory of Population," 57 and 58 : 251-268.

Weyl, W., " Experiment in Populaton," Atlantic, 103 : 261.

——, " New Americans," Harpers, No. 129 (1914), 61s. ff.

Westropp, H. M. and Wake, C. S., *The Phallic Ideas in the Religious Antiquity.*

Whipple, G. C., *Vital Statistics*, New York, 1919.

Willcox, W. F. (Ed'r.), "International Migrations," *Natl. Bu. Econ. Research,* New York, 1929.

Willoughby, R. R., "Fertility and Parental Intelligence," *Am. J. Psychol.,* 40: 671-2.

Winthrop, R. C., *Life and Letters of John Winthrop*, Boston, 1869.

Wolfe, A. B., *Reading in Social Problems*, New York, 1916.

——, "Is There a Biological Law of Population Growth?", *Q. J. Econ.,* August, 1927.

Women's City Club of New York, "Child and Youthful Marriages in New York Count."

Woodruff, A. A., *Foundations of Biology*, New York, 1922.

——, C. E., *Expansion of Races*, New York, 1909.

Woods, E. C., "Heredity and Opportunity," *Amer. Jour. Social,* 26: 1-21, 146-161.

Wooley, C. L., *The Sumerians*, Oxford, 1929.

Woolston, H. B., "Limit of American Population," *Social Forces,* 4: 5-16.

Wright, H., *Population*, New York, 1923.

Young, A., *Farmers Letter*, edition of 1728.

Yule, G. U., *The Fall of the Birth Rate*, London, 1920.

INDEX

237

Mac Iver, R. M., 204
Malthus, D., 31
Malthus, T. R., 11, 12, 29, 30-54, 57, 59-61, 65, 79, 135, 195, 204, 208, 210, 213
Marriage rate, 183, 184
Marshall, A., 52
Marshall, F. H. A., 128n, 129
Marx, K., 42, 48
McFall, R. J., 104, 105
Mendel, L. B., 67
Menstruation, 125-129
Merchantilists, population doctrines of, 25, 27
Migration, 155-164
Mill, J. S., 203
Mun, T., 27

Negro survival, 148-151
Neo-Malthusianism, 47, 56
Newsholm, A., 180
New York City, infant mortality, 142
Nitte, F. S., 54

Optimum population, 72, 73
Over-population, 153
Over-propagation, 11, 12, 15, 119, 121
Osborn, T. B., 67

Patten, S. N., 50
Patterson, E. M., 105
Pearl, R., 58, 64-71, 112, 167, 174, 202, 203, 217
Petty, W., 26
Pierson, N. G., 55, 56, 73
Pitt, W., 32
Polar regions as a source of food, 107
Population, optimum, 72, 73, 89-94; prehistoric, 89-94; socialist doctrines of, 47, 48
Population growth, Malthusian theory of, 35, 36, 39; mode of, 65, 66

Poverty, Malthusian theory of, 34, 39
Progress, 83, 88, 95, 218; defined, 188

Reproduction, 115-122
Ricardo, D., 12, 21, 49, 54, 203
Roberts, L. J., 98
Ross, E. A., 130, 209-212

Sadler, M. T., 46, 69
Say, J-B., 107, 108
Sea, as a source of food, 105, 106
Senior, N. W., 33, 204
Smith, A., 27-29
Smith, J. R., 100
Socialist population doctrine, 47-49
Spencer, H., 121, 130, 195
Standard of Living, defined, 14, 15; effect upon migrations, 161
Sterility, 125, 126
Struggle for existence, 80-89, 96-108
Subsistence, minimum of, 96n, 96-108
Sweeney, J. S., 71, 72, 204
Swinburne, J., 74

Taussig, F. W., 51, 52

Under-nourishment, consequences of, 97, 98
Unicellulars, growth of, 109
United Kingdom, condition of population, 102
United States, birth rate, 171; condition of population, 102-104; infant mortality, 140

Walker, F. A., 162, 163
Wallace, A. R., 11, 13
Wealth, defined, 22, 23
Wilcox, W. F., 134, 157
World population, growth of, 99
Wright, H., 50, 77, 78
Young, A., 46